P9-ASE-822

Beginning with Brandon's Interest

STUDIES IN INCLUSIVE EDUCATION
Volume 9

Scope
This series addresses the many different forms of exclusion that occur in schooling across a range of international contexts and considers strategies for increasing the inclusion and success of all students. In many school jurisdictions the most reliable predictors of educational failure include poverty, Aboriginality and disability. Traditionally schools have not been pressed to deal with exclusion and failure. Failing students were blamed for their lack of attainment and were either placed in segregated educational settings or encouraged to leave and enter the unskilled labour market. The crisis in the labor market and the call by parents for the inclusion of their children in their neighborhood school has made visible the failure of schools to include all children.

Drawing from a range of researchers and educators from around the world, Studies in Inclusive Education will demonstrate the ways in which schools contribute to the failure of different student identities on the basis of gender, race, language, sexuality, disability, socio-economic status and geographic isolation. This series differs from existing work in inclusive education by expanding the focus from a narrow consideration of what has been traditionally referred to as special educational needs to understand school failure and exclusion in all its forms. Moreover, the series will consider exclusion and inclusion across all sectors of education: early years, elementary and secondary schooling, and higher education.

Beginning with Brandon's Interest

Albert Osei
Ontario Institute of Studies in Education at the
University of Toronto
Vaughan Centre for Autism, Canada

SENSE PUBLISHERS
ROTTERDAM/BOSTON/TAIPEI

A C.I.P. record for this book is available from the Library of Congress.

ISBN: 978-94-6091-300-6 (paperback)
ISBN: 978-94-6091-301-3 (hardback)
ISBN: 978-94-6091-302-0 (e-book)

Published by: Sense Publishers,
P.O. Box 21858,
3001 AW Rotterdam,
The Netherlands
http://www.sensepublishers.com

Printed on acid-free paper

DEDICATION

Bird songs

*Oh, there's music in the forests
And there's music in the glen,
As the birds are warbling greetings
To the spring that's come again.*

*All their piping is so merry
That the woodlands seem to ring,
With the praises of the birdsongs
For the coming of the spring.*

*Join the joyous woodland chorus
And raise high your voice in cheer,
Join the birdsongs in thanksgiving
For the springtime of the year!*

From *Spring Fun for Kids* by Bethany Roberts' (2008)

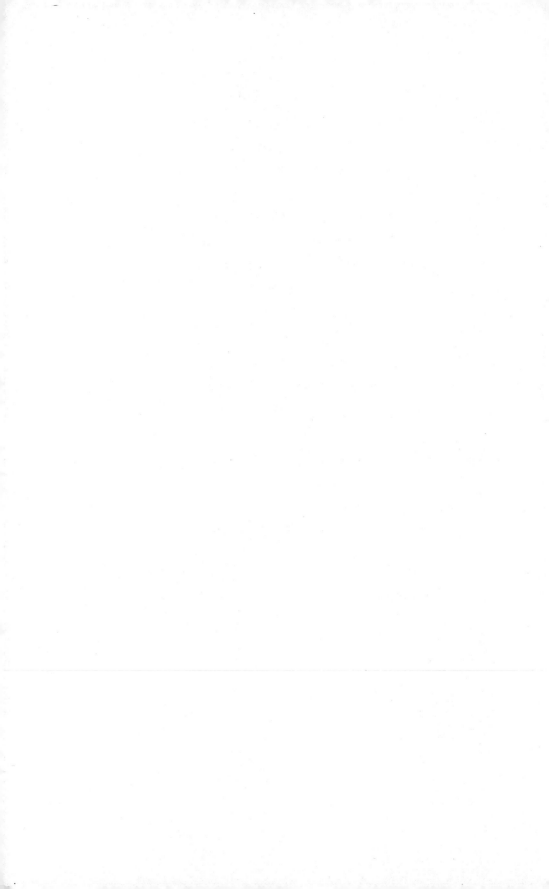

TABLE OF CONTENTS

APPENDIXES

ABSTRACT

When Brandon was diagnosed with global developmental delay (GDD) and pervasive developmental disorder (PDD) in 1997, he was found to be severely limited in social, learning, and language skills. Consequently, it was difficult for him to communicate with people and have them understand his expressions. He showed less interest in what others were doing but as his primary caretaker and communicator, I learned to communicate with him and understand him. Utilizing his profound interest in birds, music, and gardens as centers for teaching and learning, he has been able to develop social and academic relationships with his teachers and peers.

Drawing from a blend of phenomenological and narrative approaches, this study explores a father's experience with the influence of nature and music on one autistic child's learning experience. Using observations and journal writing, I have been able to record Brandon's conversations, his outdoor learning and reading activities, my interpretations and our collaborative efforts to make meaning of his expressions.

Central to this study is Hawkins (1682), Head (1997), Turner and Freedman's (2004) notion of nature and music as mediums for teaching and learning. Developing this study within the context of education, and from my own experience as a father researcher gives credence to the study in a way that will hopefully allow educators, parents, respite programmers, and professional service providers to take advantage of the idea that the autistic child, regardless of his or her differences, can be successful socially and academically.

This study consolidates the knowledge that nature and music are universal educational tools that can help autistic children to learn to improve on their differences.

ACKNOWLEDGEMENT

In February 1997, at age three, Brandon was diagnosed with pervasive developmental disorder (PDD). Brandon's situation changed the way we lived our lives; as a result, we learned and discovered our new selves in the world. There have been several people and service agencies that have made our experiences with autism worthwhile. First, I would like to thank almighty God for giving us hearts, minds, and skills that can tirelessly care for a person living with PDD. I thank my family: my wife Doris, and my three children, Valerie, Brandon and Chelsea who have supported each other and our entire family to help deal with the exigencies of autism. This note of appreciation extends to our extended family of professional service providers, special educators, and community care groups that have provided special support services for Brandon since he was diagnosed with autism. Through our collective experiences, we have accomplished our task of supporting Brandon from his early childhood impairment to a liberated young adulthood.

Thank you, Brandon, for showing courage, perseverance and sharing your experiences with a crippling human developmental disorder that has left many children isolated from their loved ones. Brandon's interest in nature and music not only taught us how to develop a constructive dialogue with him after several communicative approaches had failed to appeal to his interest in education, but his enthusiasm for nature and music helped us to understand his unique social and cognitive abilities.

My gratitude goes to David Selby who opened up my academic life to the world of Global Education and George Sefa Dei whose outstanding work in cross-cultural and inclusive education has helped me endure the rigorous life at OISE. I appreciate very much the support from Michael Connelly for welcoming me to the Narrative Inquiry Community Seminar (NICS). NICS helped me to relive and retell my storied life and provided me with the narrative tools for developing a textual account of my lived experiences. I have a great debt of gratitude to my many friends at OISE, whose encouragement and insights helped me to learn about many great new ideas. The NICS family gave me the opportunity to meet very intelligent and insightful people and I am grateful. I thank Kathy Bickmore for her patience, humor and intellect; she worked tirelessly to help me improve my academic work skills. A special thank you goes to Joseph Ducharme, Elizabeth Smyth, and Njoki Wane who reviewed and supported me throughout the development of the study.

My thesis committee is comprised of not only first class academic scholars, but also caring individuals who actively helped me along my academic journey from conceiving my dissertation topic to completing it. My academic work at OISE would not have been completed without the colossal support I received from my thesis committee. I am greatly indebted to Linda Cameron, my thesis supervisor, for her counselling, motivation and guidance at times when the future of the work was in doubt. Linda will forever be remembered for encouraging me to work hard. I am very thankful for Maria José Botelho's encouragement and for the feedback she provided. Without her, many of the words and ideas in this scholarship would not have come to fruition. My gratitude goes also to David Booth for providing the road map to bring this academic work into being.

My deepest gratitude goes to the Geneva Centre for Autism for providing me with academic as well as material resources for completing my field study. This study has also benefited enormously from workshops and conferences organized by the Geneva Centre. My appreciation goes to the Lorna Jackson Public School for inviting me to join the special education class visit to the Toronto Zoo. During my visit to the Zoo, I gained enormous experience about how Brandon and his peers interact with animals in captivity.

I could not have finished this work without the moral support from friends such as Imri Young, Shaibu Gariba, Peter Macharthy, Alex Asamoah, Ian Eldon Adams, and Sonia Baruzzo. I have shared interesting ideas and learned many creative things from this group of friends. I thank Willis Williams and Dorian Nicholson for critiquing and editing my work. I have enjoyed working with them and without their insights I might not have been able to complete the dissertation. My special thanks goes to the faculty members and staff at the Department of Curriculum, Teaching and Learning (CTL) and the Students Services of the Ontario Institute of Studies of Education at the University of Toronto.

Finally, I express my gratitude to people that I feel I have not thanked enough for all the things they have done for me. My mother, Madam Yaa Tiwaah, and my father, Albert Wireko Osei (deceased), have devotedly encouraged me to pursue higher learning and without their intuition and support, I doubt I could have earned a PHD. I thank my brothers, Victor Yaw Osei and Lawrence Osei, for encouraging me and showing great interest in my work. Last but not least, my deepest appreciation goes to my wife, Doris Amankwah- Osei. Without her, this dissertation would not have been possible. I dedicate this dissertation to her and my children.

CHAPTER 1

THE BIRTH OF EXPERIENCE

Where the Story Began

Our living with children in natural situations of parenting and teaching is much less characterized by constant choice and rational decision making than theories of the teacher as "reflective practitioner" and "deliberative decision maker" have made us believe. Rather, in concrete and particular contexts we much more accurately are involved in actions immediately and directly. (Van Manen, 1990, p. 156)

It was April 1, 1994. My mother was the first person to wake up at 5 a.m. and she began her customary morning prayer. I heard her voice through the wall. It was like a spiritual melody, a ritual reminder for the rest of the house to begin our prayers. At about 6:25 a.m., the house cleaning had started, Doris (my wife) cleaned the kitchen and I did dishwashing and vacuuming. The noise had grown louder and awakened Brandon and Chelsea but Valerie was still asleep. At about 7:05 a.m., the children's favourite television program was on. I was almost finished with cleaning the carpet in Brandon's room when I heard my mother's footsteps rubbing on the hardwood floor, walking to the living room to join the children. At first, I thought television had attracted her attention but I was wrong. I heard my mother's low and unthreatening voice calling me to the living room where the children were. She pointed to Brandon and said, "Brandon is rocking, his eyes gazing and not responding to my overtures, these behavioral characteristics are abnormal with a child at his age!" (Osei, Journal entry, 1994).

Was she right? Was this informal, loving diagnosis real? My mother's observation jarred me into facing what had so long been kept silent, a hidden, unspoken terrible fear.

Brandon had been observed and checked by the family doctor who had said that he was fine. I thought that if Brandon's rocking and eye gazing were health problems the family doctor would have made a recommendation. The fear wrenched through my heart and head. With such thoughts lingering in my mind and still in denial, I assumed that his behaviours were really nothing serious. My mother's words kept ringing in my head.

Even though she has no formal education, her experience with raising six children makes it difficult to ignore her observation. I said to myself if what I had observed is a disability as opposed to behavioral difference then he has been separated from his family for quite a while (Osei, Journal entry, 1994). At this time, several issues crisscrossed my mind. The social labelling and discrimination that are frequently meted at people living with impairments would present a colossal burden to his socialization and education. Such thoughts were among the many things that filled my eyes with tears and compounded my fathering.

This autobiographical account represents the experiences that I have acquired fathering a child with one of the most complex disorders in developmental science. It is also about a family's unrelenting quest for acquiring problem-solving skills to help one autistic child to overcome difficulties in school and have access to what he deserves to develop progressively like his typical developing peers. I come to this study not as a teacher but as a parent, scientist, educator, and disability rights advocate. I also bring to bear my fathering experience in educating one child with autism to achieve his educational goal. On a scholarly note, this study represents a personal life story of a father's search and found educational activities that elicit the educational interest of a young autistic student after deciphering several inconsistent, contradictory and problematical pedagogies that have refused to address Brandon's social and cognitive needs and what he deserves to be creative and productive in school.

This study is conducted in Toronto, Ontario, Canada. We began observing and documenting our experience with Brandon's language, social and cognitive skills from the day he was born and throughout his schooling. My interest in Brandon's learning experience is motivated by my own experience in nature and music education. I also have been influenced by my father's parenting skills I experienced as a child growing up on the farm and educated in an urban school system.

Through love, patience, caring, commitment, and discipline I have found nature and music as the most appropriate ways for developing Brandon's interest in learning new concepts and skills. This is our story and now let me introduce you to Brandon.

BRANDON

Brandon started to attend nursery school at Mini Skool in Brampton, Ontario, six months after his birth and he interacted positively with people around him. A careful observation of his early interests confirmed that he was a happy child with an inquisitive mind. His curiosity about his environment began to unfold after the third month of his development. He introduced us to his social and cognitive abilities by demonstrating his fascination for the outdoors and like many children of his age; he explored everything that came in his way. His interest in outdoor play became more evident as he grew older. For example, his attraction to songbirds, dolphins, and his interest in exploring the bushes, flowers, and other outdoor activities were some of the early signs that clearly communicated his interest in nature.

At six months of age, Brandon could clearly communicate his interest in birds such as chickadees. He demonstrated aptitude in chickadee language by imitating their vocalizations and singing with them. Whenever, he was in the park his energy was high and his attention was focused on chickadees and chickadee improvisation. His favourite indoor activity was to listen to music on the radio or the television such that he would practice the songs he learned. He demonstrated passion for plants, flowers, vines, and trees crowned with evergreen leaves where chickadees nest. His favourite place at the park was the fruit gardens where berries and fruits of all types grow. He liked the apple trees located at the northern section of the park behind our home because he would often find flocks of chickadees resting and nesting. At age three, Brandon could distinguish differences in chickadee vocalizations. He also showed deep interest in finches, woodpeckers, titmice, and nuthatches because of their acrobatic skills. His initial visit to Marineland in July 1996 indicated that his interest in nature extended far beyond birds and gardens.

Brandon's interests at home followed him to the classroom. His developmental report completed by his nursery school teacher in March 1996 suggested that he likes to sing and listen to songs. At age three, he demonstrated that he could respond to instructions in English and vernacular languages (Twi). His bilingualism helped him to process information at home as well as in school but his receptive and expressive languages developed slowly (Yanchyshyn, 1998). At age four, his social and cognitive developments were slow because he showed significant delay in his speech and language skills. For example, he could only communicate in single words and phrases. His echolalia was evident because he frequently repeated words that were said to him but over the years his repetitive behaviour reduced and he could say short sentences using the pronoun "I" and "we" for plurals (Handley-Derry, 1997). From January 1997 to September 1999, Brandon attended preschool at Margaret Fletcher Day-care. In February 1997, Brandon's social and cognitive differences became a concern to his nursery school teachers, which led to his referral and to be examined by a paediatrician in behavioral differences in children. Subsequently, he was diagnosed with global developmental delay (GDD) in February 1997, followed by diagnosis of pervasive developmental disorder (PDD) in December 1997. His curiosity in nature became important pedagogic and dialogic tools after his autism diagnosis.

When Brandon reached five years of age, he began junior kindergarten at the Huron Street Public School. His interest in nature play remained and he continued to indulge in self play and repetitive behaviours. Interestingly, over the years, he continued his interest in music and nature play. For example, he enjoyed outdoor activities such as bird watching, mimicking sounds with birds and taking nature walks. However, he continued to have difficulty in developing personal care skills such as toiletry. Brandon underwent a number of assessments from Grades 1 to 8. His Ontario Student Record (OSR) indicated that on the cognitive realm of development, he enjoyed reading and listening to music; he had incredible mental capacity for memorizing musical lyrics, creative dancing and he commanded an extensive repertoire of names of people and places; he could count to 30 and identify objects in pictures; and he could recognize differences in colours and words in print; he could produce sets of objects to 10. In the area of socialization he enjoys dancing and could sing to or with others (Yanchyshyn, 1998).

Brandon visited the Hospital for Sick Children for communication and hearing assessments and the evaluations were completed in April 1997. The results suggested that his speech reception, warble and pure tone thresholds were consistent with his gross normal bilateral hearing (Papaioannou, 1997). However, Brandon's development and educational needs presented serious challenges to his education. For this reason, the Toronto District School Board and the York Region District School Board of Education on a number of occasions, as his education demanded, consulted with a number of professional service organizations from June 1998 to January 2007.

Brandon's initial behavioral assessment was completed by the Toronto District School Board District-Wide Special Education Resource Service for Autism in December 1998 (Yanchyshyn, 1998). According to the resource teacher report, Brandon was a visual learner who communicated mainly through gestures and postures and the school was asked to provide him with a one-on-one behavioral support to help him integrate successfully in classroom activities. It was also recommended that curricular activities should focus on advancing Brandon's social play competency, expressive and receptive language skills to increase his social and cognitive consciousness, to make him less dependent on others in the classroom.

At a local school team meeting, it was suggested that an assessment of Brandon's information processing skills was needed to help teachers develop curricular activities that will address his educational needs. A behavioral assessment was completed in March 1999 by the Toronto District School Board (Cole, 1999). The behavioral evaluation indicated that Brandon learns best when classroom instructions and words are put into a song. The Toronto District School Board Health Support Services completed occupational therapeutic assessment relative to Brandon's fine motor skills and the examiners recommended that his hand preference was not yet established and that he lacked requisite motor skills for printing and drawing. This was followed by the Toronto District School Board's speech and language assessments that were completed in November 2002 (Ling, 2002). The report suggested that Brandon showed interest in interacting with adults more than his peers. It was also observed that he sometimes communicated in words that did not make sense and that many of his utterances were in single words or phrases. Brandon's most recent behavioral assessment was completed in January 2007. It was reported that he was a sociable young man who was very conscious of his learning environment and shows interest in working with adults. Furthermore, it was suggested that he benefited from verbal instructions and nature- based activities such as sand play and nature walks (Boyko, 2007).

Brandon's curiosity in fruit gardens, birds and birdsongs became important learning tools after he was diagnosed with global developmental delay (GDD) and pervasive developmental disorder (PDD) in 1997. The clinical definition of GDD suggests that the child has impairment in key areas of development. One indicator is if a child demonstrates difficulty using language or words at an attained age where typical developing children are expected to develop normal language (Carman et al., 2006). According to the American Academy of Neurology and the Child Neurology Society of America, "between 40,000 and 120,000 U.S., and Canadian children are born each year with global developmental delay" (Alementi, 2003).

While incurable, early testing and diagnosis could provide more accurate information about GDD and help researchers to determine the cause of the disorder, and assist physicians and parents in developing a plan for treatment. GDD is prevalent in one to three percent of children less than 5 years of age. It is defined as significant delay in two or more of these developmental areas: gross/fine motor, speech/language, cognition, social/personal, and activities of daily living.

At age four, Brandon's social and cognitive differences became clearer and as a result he was formally diagnosed with PDD. At the time of Brandon's GDD and PDD diagnoses there was little information available for accessing appropriate therapeutic or educational services that could help him improve his social and cognitive differences. As a result, we were motivated to draw information from experiences we have developed earlier in his childhood that had helped us as parents to dialogue with him after his teachers and several professional service providers have made unsuccessful efforts to communicate with him. To date, there is no generalized accepted therapy that could help him to improve on his developmental differences.

Our most important experience as parent/educators began when Brandon entered Grade One at the Huron Public School. We (Doris and I) met with the Identification, Placement and Review Committee (IPRC) met on June 1998, to discuss Brandon's extra classroom support and transitional strategies (Osei, 2008). The Team interviewed us for an hour about our experience with Brandon's learning skills. We informed the IPRC Team about the important contribution nature and music play in Brandon's educational experience.

After the IPRC interview of Doris and I, the Team requested Brandon to be assessed by a district-wide resource consultant because the Board had observed that there was a need for consultation regarding transitional planning and classroom placement. The initial district -wide special education service examination was based on structured and non-structured activities conducted to assess Brandon's social and cognitive competences.

The examination consisted of both indoor and outdoor assignments and the indoor activities included listening to music play and circle drawing, while the outdoor program focused on drawing in the sand, and climbing and swing play activities with peers (Yanchyshyn, 1998). After failing to demonstrate his ability to work independently and meet other classroom expectations in areas of communication and personal care, the examiners recommended a special education class for Brandon with support from the Hanen Speech and Language Services for Kids. It was also agreed between the school and our family that the school would put in place an intensive behavioral support to make Brandon less dependent on adult supervision.

The Board recognized that Brandon was a visual learner who communicated with people through gestures and movement but he sometimes uses simple sentences or phrases to answer questions posed to him. According to the Board there was no spontaneity or reciprocal communication observed during Brandon's IPRC examination (Yanchyshyn, 1998), and they did not make it a priority to find out why Brandon refused to reciprocate language communicated to him. It was decided that the curriculum for the upcoming year was to focus on improving language development and play skills such that Brandon could interact with his teachers and peers. The Board expected the transition from day-care to community schooling to be a smooth experience. The changeover was difficult and painstaking and fell short of what the IPRC team and Brandon's parents had expected. As a result, Brandon experienced serious difficulties with his placement in community schooling.

There were several reasons attributed to the failure of the IPRC process to achieve its expected objectives. The IPRC examination was limited in scope because it focused on built play instead of nature-based activities. The testing program was squeezed into a two-hour examination session. The time allowed for the examination was limited and it made it difficult for Brandon to make any significant progress. The IPRC examiners had limited interaction with Brandon and the misstep deprived the examiners adequate information they needed to come up with educational activities that were of interest to him. The failure resulted from Brandon's lack of interest in the activity he was tested on and his examiners lack of understanding of his social and cognitive needs. The examination did not reflect Brandon's style of learning and neither did the exercise incorporate his interest in nature and music interactions. Brandon was inspired by nature and music because he learned from his interactions with nature and music, and he makes meaningful social and cognitive connections when activities are nature based. He learns best by doing.

In summary, Brandon's unique story has been the basis for developing this study and it offers rich experiences for special educators, parents, service agencies, respite workers, and professional service providers who work with children and adults with autism spectrum disorders. One of the most important contributions this study makes to special education is the influence of the experience of nature and music on one autistic child's educational experience. Brandon's unique experience and the development of this study draw from Freire's (2003) idea that "only through communication can human life hold meaning" (p. 77). While the study approaches fathering autism as a learning experience, it delves into the unique experience of a father caring for and raising a child with autism. For this reason, the study has acquired experiences that would benefit special education teachers, parents of autistic children and professional service providers who are looking for problem-solving ways for addressing the challenges autistic students face in school.

AUTISM SPECTRUM DISORDERS

According to the American Psychological Association (ASP) autism spectrum disorder (ASD) consists of a complex developmental impairment that restricts a person's ability to communicate, socially interact, and respond appropriately to one's surroundings (Minshew, 2001; Tidmarsh et al., 2003; Starr et al., 2003). Autism affects people without any preference to racial, cultural, ethnic, economic, social, or geographical orientation. It is a lifelong developmental impairment, the range and intensity of impairment varies from mild to severe. There is no known cause or cure for the neurological disorders and they affect four times as many boys than girls and they are often diagnosed at the third year of life (Geneva Center for Autism, 2005; Tager-Flusberg et al., 2001; Starr et al., 2003).

Children with autism experience social interaction difficulties and cognitive developmental delays (Tanguay, 2000; Baron-Cohen et al., 1992; Brown et al., 2001; Kuoch et al., 2003; Kohler et al., 2001). Autism presents difficult educational challenges to special education teachers (Kohler et al., 2003). However, studies on autism spectrum disorders indicate that when children with autism are exposed to primary educational programs starting as early as 2 to 3 years of age, autistic children could improve on their academic work skills (Tanguay, 2000; Baron-Cohen et al., 1992). There has been voluminous information that has emerged over the last decade with different educational activities for assisting students with autism to improve on their academic competences. McConnell (2002) suggests that a substantial part of current educational programs for advancing academic work skills of students with autism have been drawn from applied behavioural analysis (ABA) and related studies. So far, evidence suggests that available special curricular activities are limited in scope because they do not demonstrate adequate understanding of students experiences to be able make meaningful progress in appealing to their interest in education. As a result, studies have identified contemporary curricular activities as superficial and outwardly imposed on the autistic student. In this study PDDs and autism are used interchangeably to identify similarities relative to the experiences of autistic students in school.

The literature reviewed so far, suggests that there is a proliferation of research interest for information that would ultimately help educators to address the academic interest and learning needs of students with autism. Few studies have been able to lead researchers and educators to educational activities that make sense in autistic students' experiences. For this reason, there has been an ongoing debate about the need to find a way for appealing to the learning interest of autistic students (McConnell, 2002). For example, O'Brien and Pearson (2004) have dismissed the clinical approach to autism and autism education because they have observed that it compromises on the experiences of students living with autism. Traditionally, autism has been associated with learning impairment and low academic progress. Petersen (2006) argues that the social construction of disability discriminates against those without voice, such as autistic students and other students with learning impairments. Gabel (2002; 2005), Peters and Chimedza (2000) call for the recognition of individual abilities of students living impairments as a starting point for moving toward the understanding of their experiences. Collins (2000) contends that understanding a person's experiences does not require a second opinion for validating the experiences but to recognize the knowledge and standpoint as an integral part of the collective whole. In this way no one individual would consider him or herself as possessing a complete knowledge. Rather, knowledge and understanding is linked and dependent upon a community of individuals.

Foucault (1994) cautions special education teachers and psychological investigators that:

> It is natural that observation should lead to experiment, provided that experiment should question only in the vocabulary and within the language proposed to it by the things observed; its questions can be well founded only if they are answers to an answer itself without question, an absolute answer that implies no prior language, because, strictly speaking, it is the first word. (p. 108)

Here, it is understood that education suffers when one's experiences are marginalized. We also learn from Freire (2003) that human experience can not be silent nor could

7

it be described in falsehood. This means that autistic student's personal experiences are an important vehicle for helping students, educators, parents and professional providers build a compendium of information to advance special education research.

Researchers and educators have not paid adequate attention to the influence of nature and music on autistic students' academic work skills. Brandon's interest in nature and music has revealed his academic interest, exceptional learning abilities, and communication skills. As Gabel (2002), Collins (2000), O'Brien and Pearson (2004) have observed, it is only when contemporary studies are able to recognize autistic student's experiences would it be possible for the multiple identities imposed on them to be addressed. The focus of this study is to explore the experience of the influence of nature and music on Brandon's learning skills as a way of developing information that would help researchers, parents, and educators who work and provide support for autistic children to meet their everyday challenges in school and at home. I expect that such information would help to address some critical issues relating to Brandon's learning differences and how the information would help others.

NATURE AND MUSIC AS EDUCATIONAL EXPERIENCE

We learn from Hawkins' (1682), Head (1997), Turner and Freedman (2004) that nature has musical qualities capable of influencing humans and animal species to develop musical minds. The studies have attributed the invention of music to nature and natural sound. The revelation explains why Brandon is fascinated with nature and music and why he learns best when activities are nature and music based. For example, Brandon's interest in birds and birdsongs provide a clue to why he developed obsessive interest in music, dance, singing and reading to improve his socialization and learning skills.

Several theorists have identified the important relationship between nature and music (including musical sounds in nature, the blending of natural sound and music, music inspired by nature) and their influences on education. Head (1997), Turner and Freedman (2004) have observed the important role birdsongs play in capturing human interest in music. Head's study of birdsongs has revealed that not only do birdsongs influence human interest in music and music learning, relatively; birdsongs are the origin of music and music learning. Hawkins (1682) has observed that:

> The voices of animals, the whistling of the winds, the fall of waters, the concussions of bodies of various kinds, not to mention the melody of birds, as they contain in them the rudiments of harmony, may easily be supposed to have furnished the minds of intelligent creatures with such ideas of sound, as time, and the accumulated observation of succeeding ages, could not fail to improve into a system. (Cited in Head, 1997, p. 12)

Hawkins discusses how nature and music have influenced human learning long before music became an art form. Hawkins argues that music and music learning are found everywhere in nature. Similarly, Turner and Freedman argue that birdsongs influence human learning. Hawkins, Head, Turner and Freedman contend that birdsongs are the foundation of music and music learning.

Although, studies have found nature and music important tools for developing instructional strategies for children with learning differences, few studies have been able demonstrate how to advance the influence of nature and music education on children with autism beyond the therapeutic realm to the teaching and learning domain, where these students could acquire social and intellectual skills to improve their educational development. For example, Halder (2006) and Louv (2006) approach nature as a therapeutic site while Shepard (1982) and Hutchison (1998) see nature as the essence of our humanity that needs to be explored and learn from to understand the complexity of our human nature. One of the profound weaknesses in studies on nature and music education is the disproportionate attention given to nature and music as therapeutic tools for treating behavioral differences in children with autism. The inadequate emphasis given to teaching and learning strategies in nature and music education that are capable of influencing children with autism to acquire the social and cognitive skills they deserve to develop successfully in school has brought about tensions in nature and music education research. This study explores ways of advancing teaching and learning strategies in nature and music education that helps children with autism to learn and improve their skills.

CONNECTIONS TO NATURE AND NATURE LEARNING

Drawing from Hawkins' (1682), Head's (1997), Turner and Freedman's (2004) ideas of nature, nature offers children with a rich experience of the world of music. Smith-Sebasto and Semrau (2004) argue that when children are adequately exposed to nature, it encourages their curiosity and improves their critical thinking skills. Palmberg and Kuru (2004) assert that nature experiences provide children with self-confidence, a sense of safety and the willingness to learn new skills. However, studies suggest that special education researchers have not paid adequate attention to the contribution nature offers autistic students in education. McConnell (2002) has observed that current autism studies do not offer adequate information about productive ways of organizing educational activities capable of eliciting the interest of autistic pupils. Palmberg and colleagues (2000), Shepardson (2005), Kola-Olusanya (2005) have recommended community alternatives such as nature based activities as an important pedagogic tool for facilitating academic competence skills in children. Laa and family (2008) and Louv (2006) have taken a more pragmatic approach for addressing learning differences in autism by recommending autistic children to be involved in nature based activities such as bird watching and horse riding as a means for improving their sense of self and community, and develop confidence as a way for improving their social and academic work skills. In a recent article published by the Canadian Press (2006) describing the growing influence of bird watching and horse riding on children. Bird watching and horse riding have had enormous influence on child development. Unfortunately, researchers have been reluctant in exploring the contribution human interaction with birds and horses have had on autism and the education of autistic children.

We also learn from Smith-Sebasto and Semrau (2004) that children's adequate exposure to nature could improve their confidence and advance their intellectual skills.

Palmberg and Kuru (2000) attribute the lack of children's nature literacy to researchers' failure to develop adequate information about nature that could be introduced to children in a variety of learning environments. Louv (2006) has observed that nature inspires creativity in children. Little is known about the influence of nature on autistic children's learning and creative skills.

CONNECTIONS TO MUSIC AND MUSIC LEARNING

The study approaches music as "an agreeable sound; vocal, instrumental, or mechanical sounds having rhythm, melody, or harmony, and the science or art of ordering tones or sounds in succession, in combination, and in temporal relationships to produce a composition having unity and continuity" (Music, 2008, p. 1). The lexicon interpretation of music encouraged me to explore Brandon's fascination with birds and birdsongs as a way for developing this field study. My examination of music as "an agreeable sound" suggested that Brandon's interest in birdsongs and music supported Hawkins', Head's, Turner and Freedman's notions of music as originating from birdsongs. Austern (2001) and Head (1997) argue that music is a universal cultural expression that serves as a point of connection between humans and the natural world.

Miranda (2004) argues that music could create a community of learners by bringing together individual experiences to improve teacher practice and students' academic growth. Marjoribanks and Mboya (2004) have jointly observed that a student's interest in music positively influences his or her learning and goal orientation. Hidi and Harackiewicz (2000) have indicated that if there were a better understanding of the relationships among students' music learning skills, expectations, and interests, teachers would be better prepared to help advance students academic work skills. For example, Butzlaff (2000) contends that music education could advance children's reading and writing skills. We also learn from Ainley, Hidi, and Berndorff (2002) that for teachers to improve their music teaching practices they need to understand students' interest and musical skills. They argue that teachers could expand students interests in music to other related subject areas if they have adequate information of students music interest and goal orientations.

NATURE AND MUSIC AS A RESEARCH FIELD

My interest in nature and music learning began before Brandon was born and a reflection on my experience made it possible for me to gain knowledge of some important information for helping Brandon to acquire the learning tools he deserves to succeed in school. The study of the influences of nature and music is closely connected to how knowledge is acquired in naturalistic settings. The study reveals how Brandon developed academic work skills from his interaction with birds and birdsongs.

Much is written about the difficulty autistic children face in developing language, social and intellectual skills. There is inadequate information relative to the influence of nature and music on autistic children. For example, Louv (2006) has recognized the important contribution nature makes to the social and intellectual development of children with attention deficit hyperactive disorder (ADHD) and other impairments. However, few studies have been able to investigate the experiences autistic students encounter in their interactions with the natural world.

Not much information is available about autistic children's experiences in music. Exkorn's (2005) concept of music therapy for autistic children focuses on how autistic children develop listening and play skills in controlled environments. We also learn from Cohen's (1980) multiple intelligence concepts, which explain how autistic children develop limited skills in music. However, that study fails to inform readers about how autistic children acquire music skills in non-clinical settings.

This study attempts to provide evidence about how nature and music had influenced one autistic student's learning skills. It is not about how Brandon learned music but rather how he learns through music, using music as a vehicle for learning. For example, nature and music influenced Brandon's social and academic skills. His interest in music motivated him to develop dance skills. Dancing became a means for Brandon to socialize with his teachers and peers. His classmates were interested to see him dance to his favourite songs. Dancing helped him to communicate with his teachers and peers. Boyko (2007) reported that Brandon received praises from his teachers and peers whenever he dances in class, and it encouraged him to pursue other classroom task such as listening to music and singing to his classmates.

Consideration should also be given to the semiotic and aesthetic meaning of nature and music learning. Brandon's fascination with nature and music helped him to express himself in authentic and reliable way that made dancing interesting and rewarding for him. Using phenomenological methods such as observations, stories, conversations, journal entries, artefacts and pictures, the study developed insights in the complex ways nature and music influenced Brandon's reading, singing, dancing, drawing, and socializing skills. The study also addresses the gap in the research literature about autistic students and their experiences with nature and music.

WHY NATURE AND MUSIC LEARNING?

Nature and music learning address one of the most important aspects of Brandon's experience with autism. I attempt in this study to fill a significant gap in knowledge by providing information of how a father, in the context of the family, improves his parenting practice. Turner and Freedman (2004) have observed that nature and music serve as a connection between the social and intellectual worlds. For example, Cohen (1980) and Flohr (1985) have found children's improvisations as an important area for helping children to expand their music learning skills. They argue that children's improvisations in their early developmental stages provide a clue to why many children develop creative musical mind. Brophy (1998) has observed that the critical stage of children's musical transformative skills begins from ages six through nine and the progression slows down after age nine. These findings are consistent with studies conducted by Vaughan (1973), Webster (1977) and Kiehn (2003) suggesting that the ability to understand children's creative skills in music begins from their music improvisations. Birds and birdsongs help transform Brandon's early music improvisations to creative singing, listening and dance skills, and these skills became dialogic and pedagogic tools for improving his classroom skills.

Clinical studies have been conducted on music as a form of therapy for improving autistic children's social and cognitive skills and how these skills could be developed to advance their academic skills (Exkorn, 2005; Cohen, 1998). The limited information about autistic students' experiences in nature and music has created a serious problem for educators about how to help autistic students to develop academic skills through nature and music. For example, there is limited information about autistic children's music improvisations, creativity, and listening skills, and how this might influence social and intellectual skills. The challenge to contemporary studies is the difficulty to address autistic students' learning needs and diverse skills in established concepts. This study discusses Brandon's improvisations with birds and birdsongs and how his interest helped to improve his social and academic skills. The experience acquired from this study is not represented in contemporary literature and it provides educators, parents and professional providers the research they need to advance autistic students nature and music skills.

IMPLICATIONS OF NATURE AND MUSIC LEARNING

The study of the influence of nature and music emphasizes the importance of one autistic child's experience engaging in nature and music learning has been used to develop a textual meaning of the phenomenological experience. Brandon's interest in nature and music is consistent with Turner and Freedman's assertion that music is an original element of nature and it provides a connection between humans and the natural world. What is it that so fascinates Brandon that he could stay engaged when music and nature are present? What attracts him so deeply? What motivates his learning? What if teachers used music and nature to capitalize on Brandon's capacity to learn, to relate, to respond?

In considering the semiotic and aesthetic aspects of nature and music learning, Kruse and Card (2004) and Bizerril (2004) have observed that when children are adequately exposed to nature they develop nature literacy more than children with less nature interactions. Custodero and Johnson-Green (2003) remind readers of what they describe as the "systems view of the musical child" (p. 103). They argue that in order to fully understand the musical child, there is more to consider in terms of how children learn through music, there is also the influence of a music-rich environment, which offers a comprehensive view of how children learn through music.

Learning from nature and music offers a premise for understanding Brandon's classroom behaviour. For parents and educators of young autistic children who are concerned about children's lack of communication, learning, listening and attentive skills, nature and music learning offers Brandon a social and intellectual environment that help him to address his academic work challenges. Kruse and Card (2004) and Bizerril (2004) tell us that when children are exposed to continuous, repeated nature learning they develop advanced nature literacy skills. The observation is supported by Louv's (2006) argument that human mental, physical, and spiritual well-being have direct association with nature. Exkorn (2005) has also observed that music can improve children's physical, mental, and social functioning skills, while Custodero and Johnson-Green (2003) have also observed that music and music learning improves children's behaviour and academic work skills.

Studies have recognized the important contribution music makes to the educational development of the autistic child. However, little is known about the influence of nature and music on children with autism. In this dissertation, I want to describe Brandon's experience with and through nature and music.

CONNECTING NATURE AND MUSIC TO OTHER FIELDS

Nature and music learning provide Brandon's educators, professional service providers and parents a broad range of support for addressing his social and learning needs. Nature and music learning provide Brandon's teachers knowledge of how he feels, think and learn. For example, when Brandon was unhappy in the classroom, nature walks and listening to music are dialogic tools for appealing to his interest, attentive listening and performance skills. Nature and music learning has also helped professional service providers to avoid rigid interpretation of Brandon's learning differences. Nature and music serve as entry points for professional service providers to develop services and professional practices that address his social and learning needs. As parents, nature and music learning offered us a way for reaching Brandon, whenever we wanted to teach him skills that he deserves to succeed at home and in school.

Dudley-Marling (2004) strengthens the problem-solving tool with a critique of the concept of "individualism" in education, which holds individuals accountable for both their learning success and failures. According to Dudley-Marling, learning and learning problems are situated not in the heads of individuals but in the learning environment. In order to advance education, he argues, society must move beyond the social construction of knowledge and embrace progressive human interactions and activities as a way for solving problems in education. Varenne and McDermott (1999) have observed many specialists assume that a disability renders a person incompetent, whether it is caused by genetic defect or lack of socialization, and they suggest that this kind of approach to education is problematic.

I approach this study with the idea that learning diversity does not make a person incompetent, but offers the learner a variety of learning opportunities based on learner's needs, preferences and expectations. In other words, reflecting on my experiences, I am able to make meaning of nature and music as learning tools for offering Brandon a place in education.

UNCOVERING A LIVED EXPERIENCE

From a phenomenological point of view, this study has made an effort to present my fathering experience with autism as it has been lived. As Van Manen has observed, to explore one's experience is to interpret the meanings of the experience in depth and to a certain degree of authenticity (Van Manen, 1990, p. 11). Much has been written about the existing conflicts in parents who study their children for the purpose of advancing knowledge in child development studies (Overton, 2003; McCabe & family, 2003). This study elucidated the essence of a fathering experience of the influence of nature and music on one autistic student's learning skills that revolved around naturally-occurring activities. The rich and authentic experiences have had a profound influence on me as well as Brandon's learning skills. However, the experience is not represented in contemporary studies and when made available, educators, researchers and parents of children living with autism would find the information important and beneficial.

CONNECTING FATHER RESEARCH TO MY FATHERING EXPERIENCE

My fathering experience with autism has been one of the most transformative experiences in my life. Brandon is a wonderful 14-year old autistic child who has been a blessing to our family because he made it possible for us to experience the world with him in extraordinary ways. Working with him has been breathtaking, rewarding and a conscious awakening experience any parent/educator would wish for because he is a very intelligent and social person to be with. Engaging him in the activities that he wants to know more about has been one of the most rewarding experiences in my life.

The complex nature of autism and related disorders forced me to reflect on the unique abilities that Brandon brings to the educator/learner interaction. Although studies have suggested that autistic children lack social and intellectual skills to make intelligible decisions, my experience with Brandon's development over the years suggests something different. I have observed that nature and music influence Brandon in unique and progressive ways. I believe that when Brandon is given the opportunity to learn he would develop exceptional social and intellectual skills that would not only advance his education but it would help educators, parents and professional service providers who have been struggling for ways to help autistic children in similar situation.

The miscommunication among stakeholders in autism research and education has contributed to severe lack of information and coordination of programs and services for children living with autism. Evidence exists (Makin, 2005a, 2005b, 2006) that experts frequently rush to judgment, and the misdiagnosis of autistic children have led parents, provincial institutions, educators and professional service providers to engage in wasteful spending of resources that could have been properly spent to reduce the burden carried by autistic children and their families. Furthermore, Makin (2005a, 2006) has observed that there is confusion between schools and autistic families about how to organize appropriate educational programs and services for autistic children in school and the problem has generated into costly litigation for the tax payer. The lack of information about how to develop educational programs and services for autistic children has made the plight of children living with autism and their families worse. For this reason, I began to think creatively about how to develop my story into text such that others may benefit from my experience.

I reviewed studies looking for parent researchers who have had a similar experience of working with their children and developing their stories into a text. I discovered that there was a long tradition of researchers that have studied ASD and related disorders and the influence on child learning. However, most of the studies on autistic children have been carried out by mother researchers and there was inadequate information about father-related studies that have studied their autistic children's development. As a result, I wanted this study to go beyond what has been written in autism research and to capture a father's experience of the influence of nature and music on one autistic child's learning experience. A reflection on my fathering experience with autism and a father who wanted to share his story to help others in similar situations resulted in my selection of the methodological framework of "father research."

MULTIPLE EXPERIENCES IN FATHER RESEARCH

From my own childhood nature experience to the ongoing inquiry into Brandon's nature and music interactions, and my desire to connect my experiences to text has made it possible for me to reflect on the narrative unity (Connelly & Clandinin, 1988) in my story and to share with readers how this story has developed over the years. I have enjoyed intergenerational experiences from my grandparents to my experience with Brandon's development. My fathering experience with autism has been fluid and consistent and my desire to share my story has helped me to understand the distinct roles I play as a father and as a researcher. As a father, I have not placed myself outside of Brandon's life as a passive observer. Rather, as an engaged father who has actively participated with keen interest in Brandon's educational experience long before this study began. My identity as a researcher and the sensitive nature of the research has brought both potential conflicts and advantages. The interpretation of Brandon's learning behaviour has been conducted in the family context and our shared experiences. I recognized that some of the findings in the study may go up against ideas developed in some mainstream studies, but what is different is the fact that as a father researcher, I have been able to reach deeper into Brandon's thinking and expectation and communicate with him candidly in a way that only Brandon and I understand, to be able to represent his story.

FROM THEORY TO PRACTICE: FATHERING AUTISM AS EDUCATION

Before my elementary education I knew that one day I would like to have my own farm. I wanted to work with farm animals, cultivate the fields, and observe plants grow. I was interested in following my ancestral occupation of growing organic food and developing productive animal husbandry to feed my family. My first visit to my father's farm provided me the opportunity to interact with farm animals such as cows, chickens, pigs, ducks, and turkeys and it also moved me closer to my interest of interacting with the natural world. The farm experience gave me a sense of security and independence and a nostalgic feeling that has been largely my early childhood nature experience.

15

Ever since Brandon was diagnosed with autism in 1997, his interest in birds and birdsongs challenged me as a father to move beyond what I already knew as a parent and educator. My usual parenting techniques such as teaching Brandon how to play with dolls, toy airplanes and trains could not appeal adequately to his interest for learning new skills. At first I thought that I was not adequately prepared to be a successful father. Brandon's complex learning skills demonstrated that I have an intelligent son with a special learning skill. My parenting challenge was to improve my parenting practice to help provide him the skills he deserves to succeed in school.

Our relationship began to change when Brandon was formally diagnosed with autism. He lost his spontaneous interactive spirit and he demonstrated less interest in the activities he had previously been fascinated about. His developmental challenge compelled me to enrol in numerous workshops and participate in several studies organized by resource agencies including the Geneva Center for Autism. In 2002, I completed a one-year training course in the applied behavioral analysis approach to transitional planning, at the Geneva Center. The program provided me knowledge of transitional planning skills and learning environments that are aimed at addressing increasing anxiety and behavioral problems. I also participated in several pilot projects with a focus on coaching parents to acquire training skills to improve their children's language, social, and cognitive skills.

When Brandon began school, I worked collaboratively with his teachers to organize classroom activities aimed at advancing Brandon's language, social and intellectual skills. I have participated as a parent volunteer in many outdoor trips that Brandon's school has undertaken. On these trips, I have provided support for Brandon's teachers about how to keep him on task and get him engaged in the outdoor activities. Although many of the skills I acquired from service agencies and my involvement in Brandon's classroom activities produced positive results that helped me as a parent and Brandon as a learner to acquire creative and productive skills, the most remarkable breakthrough for me as a parent was to revisit the nature and music activities that have appealed to Brandon's interest in the past before he was diagnosed with autism.

A reflection of my early experience of Brandon's interest in birds and birdsongs encouraged me to reintroduce nature and music parenting into my fathering practice. My interest in nature and music remained when I began graduate school. I found nature education to be a perfect fit for me to explore my experience with Brandon's learning difference. I also was able to strengthen my relationship with Brandon and to help him develop his interest in birds and birdsongs. In graduate school, I was fascinated with Turner and Freedman's (2004) idea that nature and music have the potential of transforming a child's learning skills. Their conception of nature and music motivated me to explore the social and intellectual opportunities in nature and music learning. I found out that Brandon's interest in birds and birdsongs provided him the tools he needed to gain equitable access to formal schooling. For example, Brandon's teachers, parents, peers, and professional service providers were able to develop a common language with him in nature and music activities to help him improve his social and learning skills. This is our story and it is worth telling to help people who work with children with autism to find their own voices in education.

SIGNIFICANCE OF THE STUDY

The study offers special educators, families of autistic children and professional service providers with strategies for learning with these students. The study provides experiences for engaging the educator and learner in a meaningful dialogue for the purpose of advancing one autistic student's academic work skills. For example, there is information provided about the pedagogic and dialogic content in Brandon's impulses, cues and signals that would help those people who live and work with autistic children to meet some of the challenges they face in school. This study provides readers with rich experiences of dialogic interactions and communicative expressions that are critically important for developing a productive communication with autistic students.

One of the most rewarding experiences in the study is to see how to transform one autistic child's perseverance with the things that he wants to know more about. Brandon's nature and music learning experiences provide readers dialogic and pedagogic experiences for understanding the diverse abilities in autism and autistic students, especially from ethnic minority populations who because of lack of resources have been deprived of equitable access to education. To date, many non-verbal expressions from autistic students are commonly discarded as unintelligible because listeners have difficulty interpreting them. The problem has created barriers for teachers as well as students. For this reason, the study attempts to address the pedagogic gap by taking readers through the discovery of how one autistic student found his place in school.

Although, the study is autobiographical, it addresses how one autistic student's learning needs were addressed. The study does not only offer one family's narrative experience for determining to a debilitating neurological disorder; it shows how lives were transformed from ignorance to consciousness. For respite organizers, parents and special education teachers the study provides pedagogic and dialogic places for experiencing nature's opulence and unique qualities as a means for dealing with the exigencies of autism. The study offers one autistic child's experience as a contribution to the advancement of autism research. For many autistic students who have not yet found their interest in education, the study explains how one autistic student transformed his passion for nature and music to an educational experience.

The study would benefit teachers, parents and professional providers who have found existing information inadequate relative to helping to address the learning needs of students with autism. Traditionally, many child development experts and educators have drawn from applied behavioral analysis techniques and have relied on these prescriptive therapies as a bastion for engaging autistic students. However, based on my own experience with autism and a critical review of available literature, I am convinced that there is no available therapy capable of transforming the autistic student without his or her consent. I did not arrive at this decision lightly but after working with Brandon on several exploratory and learning activities; I have found his interest in nature and music as a means for organizing pedagogy that makes sense to him. Evidence suggests that autistic students could self advocate for things that are of interest to them when given the opportunity. Findings in the study suggest that autism does not render one inadequate in education but competent in many different ways and the study challenges the typical developing world to learn more about difference.

There are inadequate studies available on parent experiences with the educational development of their autistic children. Studies have shown that there insufficient studies to help connect home training activities to classroom work to inform teachers and professional service providers practical ways for educating students with autism (McConnell, 2002; Schwartz et al., 1998; Kravitis et al., 2002; Brown et al., 2001; Kohler et al., 2001). McConnell's literary work concluded that researchers have not been able to explain the practicality and feasibility of contemporary curricular schemes for educating autistic persons to help them to develop social and cognitive competence. The idea motivating this study is to understand the experience of the influence of nature and music on one autistic students learning skills. The information would benefit students and parents as well as educators for meeting the educational needs of children living with autism.

LIMITATIONS OF THE STUDY

The study involves one research participant and that describes the limited field of the data gathering process. The focus on a single participant raises concern for the adequacy of the data gathering tools such as the absence of triangulated interviews from multiple participants that are needed to produce generalized information to support the critical arguments developed in the study. The conceptual field in autism and autistic education has been proliferated with an array of ideas and theoretical constructs. In order for a study to generalize its findings and to be taken seriously by experts, the ideas developed in the study need to be supported by multiple evidences to support its objectivity. Single case studies often lack multiple participants to support comprehensive findings.

Evidence suggests that differences in autistic behaviors vary from low to high intensity and behavioral excesses express one case may not be the same with the other. Hence, the information developed in the study may not be applicable in other situations. Another impediment is the fact that Brandon's interest in nature and music may change with time and what is important to him today may not be relevant to him in the future. Brandon's interaction with nature and music has been observed by people he knows well and a similar social and cognitive development may be different with people he does not know.

While Brandon's interest in nature and music is based on primary data collected over 14 years of consistent engagement in the data gathering process. There are many unanswered questions about how Brandon's perseveration in birds, dolphins and fruit gardens has positively influenced his learning skills. However, the long and consistent engagement in the data collection process has given strength to the findings in the study and it has also provided a compelling argument for researchers to discuss in future studies.

The father/child research relationship may have compromised the information needed to construct appropriate balance between subjectivity and objectivity.

I attempted to address the dilemma by introducing stories documented over several years before the idea for conducting the study was conceived. Although, the data was compiled in a collaborative family environment, the study lacks the potentially critical analytic lens needed to clarify and unify the subjective and objective locations of the research participants.

A GUIDE TO READING AND JUDGING THIS WORK

Although, the study is about my life as a parent/educator for one autistic child, it reveals unique experiences and situations that as a parent/educator I have shared with my son that are not represented in contemporary discourse on autism and autism education. Brandon's interest in nature and music has offered him problem-solving tools for self-advocating not only for his needs but what he deserves to succeed in school. Consequently, the reader is invited not only to experience the magic of parenting and caring for a child with social and cognitive differences but to recognize the creativity of one autistic student. In a sense, I am asking the reader to move beyond the comfort of institutionalized pedagogy and experience with me what Gabel (2002) describes as "boundless pedagogy." Boundless pedagogy identifies a way of being and becoming somebody. For Gabel, pedagogy has no boundaries when it comes to one writing his or her own story. In this study, nature and music learning identifies one autistic student's way of learning and knowing.

The stories, concepts, preoccupying questions, research method of reporting, and the data shaping the study are tools available to the reader to use to authenticate the knowledge produced in the study which aims at discovering knowledge necessary for improving one's learning differences. I approach fathering autism in the context of Van Manen's (1990) concept of parenting. I recognize the research participant as a communicative learner, a narrator and an embodied reporter, who through his impulses, gestures and utterances, has introduced me to his own ways of learning and discovering the world.

Drawing from a blend of phenomenological and narrative approaches, this study explores a father's experience of the influence with nature and music on one autistic child's learning experience. Using observations and journal writing, I have been able to record Brandon's conversations, his outdoor learning and reading activities, my interpretations and our collaborative efforts to make meaning of his expressions.

Judging this work based on the information developed in the study, readers should consider the following questions: Does the study meets the ethical standard I set out to follow? Does the central thesis of the study support the ethical standard and principles informing the study? Has the study contributed new knowledge to the field of special education? Although, my intent for pursuing this study is to share my extraordinary experiences with fathering autism and to introduce readers to one autistic child's different ways of learning and knowing, I leave room for others to review and expand on the areas that my findings may have not adequately explored.

ORGANIZATION OF THE STUDY

The study is organized into eight chapters to help readers follow the pattern of development that emerged during the research process. The organizational structure of the study offer readers a systematic progression of experiencing a life, my storied life as a parent/educator, an environmental educator, a scientist and an enthusiastic disability rights advocate who for the last 14 years has developed an entrenched interest for advancing the academic work skills of one autistic student in a cosmopolitan school for the purpose of informing and engaging the special education field in a critical debate for the advancement of education.

Chapter One introduces readers to Brandon's unique experience in education. The birth of experience describes my experience with autism and how blessed we were to have Brandon as our child. Readers are introduced to a personal narrative of motivation and determination that began the search for a learning activity that appeals to Brandon's interest in education. I attempted to contextualize my story within education to provide the reader a fervent taste of my story as I have lived it, prior to engaging in this research. The research context captures the challenges we overcame as Brandon began formal schooling.

Chapter Two is a review of the research literature, where I explore the relevant concepts and constructs that define this study. It establishes the relationship of concepts and methodological framework that provides the definitions and analytical structures for examining the influence of nature and music on Brandon's learning experience. The reservoir of information is drawn from diverse academic sources and it allowed me to provide a narrative account of my own experience along with Brandon's learning experience. Here, I explored both classic and current texts not only to scrutinize the information collected for authenticity and validity, but also to critically analyse the research to dispel any unsubstantiated and speculative findings.

Chapter Three introduces readers to the methodological framework used to develop the study. I discuss a blend of narrative studies and phenomenological hermeneutics employed in the study. I provide narrative of recruitment and collaborative account of Brandon's role in the study. I explain how the narrative stories and personal experiences collected as data for developing the study.

Within this chapter, I address the question "what is father research?" Here, I discuss my search and found pedagogic activity through father research. Although, I recognize that father research has been used by several researchers to describe fathers' experiences of their children, few of these studies have spoken about fathering experiences with autism. At essence, I discuss the important role father research has played in the development of this study as a way for advancing studies on fathering experience with autism.

Chapter Four discusses the influence of nature and music on Brandon's emotional behaviour. I provide a case study for developing this dissertation. I explore the first experience of the influence of birds, birdsongs and music on Brandon's learning skills and how the primary experience led to additional experience. I examine how zoo experience transformed Brandon's emotional behaviour into one who became an enthusiastic learner who developed social and intellectual skills through his interaction with zoo animals.

Chapter Five explores narratives of toileting training and the influence on Brandon's learning experience. I examine how interest based learning encouraged Brandon to acquire toileting skills. I provide a trajectory of Brandon's experience with birds, birdsongs and music and how the experience helped him to learn new skills.

Chapter Six provides the application of theoretical and experiential learning experience. Readers are introduced to Brandon's learning mannerisms which have been observed over 14 years of his life. The Sesame Street program provides an example of how Brandon learns from interacting with birds, birdsongs and music.

Chapter Seven highlights the findings and interpretations of ideas developed in the study. This chapter is divided into two sections as a way for reporting the contribution of father research relative to the phenomenological findings in this study. I reveal ways in which this study has brought insights into how Brandon learns. In the second section of this study, I discuss "Ecopedagogy" as a learning experience in nature that allowed this study to maintain a strong pedagogical relationship to our experiences and how they have been lived. I discuss how I gained knowledge through nature and music to address Brandon's learning challenges.

Finally, Chapter Eight provides the summary, recommendations and implications of the study. I discuss the significance of the study relating to my experience of the influence of nature and music on Brandon's learning. I make a recommendation for a national autism education strategy as a way to empower educators with a reservoir of information aimed at helping to address the social and academic inequalities in the education of children with autism spectrum disorders.

CHAPTER 2

THE LITERATURE REVIEW

Educators have had a special biographic interest in the educational lives of individuals. Educators want to gain insights in the lives of particular students' in order to understand them or help them. It is important to know where a child "is coming from" (e.g., the home background, or what it is that the child brings to school) in order to understand more sensitively where a child "is" at present, and where he or she seems "to be going." (Van Manen, 1990, p. 72)

The purpose of my literature review is to explore the relevant concepts and constructs that define this study. It also establishes the relationship of concepts and methodological framework that provides the definitions and analytical structures for examining the influence of nature and music on Brandon. My intent also is to describe the experiences as they have been lived by seeking meaning through conceptual and practical experiences to help discover relationships that might otherwise not be represented in the study.

AUTISM SPECTRUM DISORDER (ASD)

Dr. Handley-Derry's developmental assessment of Brandon suggested that Brandon was a four-year-old child who demonstrated features of a GDD "at around the two year level" (Handley-Derry, 1997). He observed that Brandon was socially interactive during the assessment procedure, which convinced him that he did not fit a typical case of autism. However, Brandon showed evidence of echolalia in his speech and his examiner concluded that Brandon's echolalia was consistent with his language development. In a follow up report completed on December 23, 2002, Handley-Derry (2002) confirmed that Brandon has GDD and PDD. PDD is one of the five disorders making up the ASD. The assessment reports showed the difficulty Brandon's prognosis presented to his examiner because of his demonstration of some exclusive abilities that did not meet the criteria of a PDD (see Glossary).

According to Minshew (2001), Tidmarsh and Volkmar (2003), and Starr and colleagues (2003), ASD consists of a complex developmental impairment that restricts a person's ability to communicate, socially interact and respond appropriately to his or her surroundings. Minshew and others have indicated that there are five disorders that make up the ASD. Studies indicate that researchers have made several unsuccessful attempts at identifying appropriate pedagogic and dialogic ways for engaging those living with ASDs in productive academic work but the outcome has been dismal. Tager-Flusberg and associates (2001), and Starr and colleagues (2003) suggest autism prognosis could improve with educational interventions from the early life to the latter years of the autistic person. Winton and Turnbull (1981),

Tanguay (2000), Baron-Cohen and associates (1992) have indicated that primary intervention programs starting from as early as 2 to 3 years of age could improve autism prognosis to help autistic students live better lives.

Although, the APA (1994) does not recognize GDD as one of the disorders making up ASD, it is described as one or more impairments in early childhood development and "implies that a child has delays in all areas of development" (Carman et al., 2006). Alementi (2003) has estimated that over 100,000 children from the United States and Canada are born each year with GDD. Carman and associates (2006) describe GDD as responsible for causing significant delays in one or more developmental areas: gross/fine motor, communication, speech/language, cognition, social/personal and daily living. This information clearly communicated differences in Brandon's learning practices, informs the study, and contributes to understanding of his learning and service needs.

A lot has been written about the important contribution educational interventions make in the advancement of the social and intellectual skills of autistic students. The revelation has led me to inquire into the role educational interventions would play in Brandon's life. I learned a lot from Lovaas's (1987) ABA pioneering work, which suggested that educational intervention could have a positive behavioral outcome for people living with autism. Lovaas and associates (1973) argue that ABA has proven to work successfully in improving the learning skills of autistic children. ABA emerges from Skinner's (1974) operant behaviour concept, which simply says that when behaviors are reinforced they are likely to reappear.

Skinner (1974) alleges that a positive reinforcer makes the behaviour that produces it stronger, and a negative reinforcer gives strength to the behaviour that suppresses it. Skinners operant condition is the most active behavioral concept applied in autism research, and many behaviourists have validated the reinforcement method as effective in helping autistic persons to improve on their behavioral deficiencies (Ferster & DeMyer, 1962; Lovaas & Newsom, 1971). Skinner (1974) observes that "the relation between a state of deprivation and the strength of appropriate behaviour is presumably due to survival value" (p. 50). Skinner connects good behaviour with social acceptance and justifies the propensity towards socially accepted behaviour as that of survival. Skinner cautions against the application of the principles of operant behaviour in exclusive environments because operant behavioral methods require the interaction of socially and culturally diverse ideas. The challenge to behavioral experts is how to make the ABA curriculum socially and intellectually inclusive to be able to address the diverse abilities and needs of children living with autism.

Lovaas and Newsom (1976) observe that ABA encompasses a variety of therapeutic intervention approaches developed by many researchers in an effort to reduce behavioral excesses of people commonly referred to as psychotic. Since Leo Kanner first discovered autism in 1943, there have been several studies undertaken by many behaviour experts to find productive ways of improving behavioural limitations associated with autism. Lovaas (1987) provides "Behavioral Treatment and Normal Education and Intellectual Functioning in Young Autistic Children" published in the Journal of Consulting and Clinical Psychology. In his article, Lovaas and associates (1971) Lovass and associates (1971), and Ferster and DeMyer (1962) have observed that behavioral studies done on autistic persons have shown that reinforcement therapies could help autistic persons to live normal lives. As Lovaas and others have alleged, "there was an emphasis on making the child look as normal as possible, rewarding him for normal behaviour and punishing his psychotic behaviour, teaching him to please his parents and us, to be grateful for what we would do for him, to be afraid of us when we were angry, and to please when we were happy. Adults were in control" (Lovaas et al., 1973, p. 135). Since Lovaas undertook his groundbreaking work, Koegel, O'Dell, and Koegel (1987) and Romanczyk (1996) studies have emerged validating the discrete trial concept and giving ABA the much needed boost it deserves.

However, scholars such as Shea (2004), Mesibov (2003) and Kasari (2002) have also undertaken similar studies to counter the arguments presented by ABA advocates by asserting that therapeutic interventions are not a clear cut solution or a magic bullet for advancing social and cognitive development in autistic students. Goode (2007) and Hodge (2005) describe the ABA education programs as socially exclusive without fervour for cultural diversity. However, Rizzolatti, Fogassi and Gallese (2006) work on "mirror neurons" challenges the clinical perceptions about autism and autistic children. The researchers point out that autistic students have innate capabilities that would allow them to self-advocate for their needs and aspirations. These findings are illuminating because we learn for the first time that the prescriptive approach to educating autistic students undermines educator/learner relationship. In fact, this research provided the impetus for strengthening the arguments against the clinical approach as a solitary solution for understanding Brandon's learning needs.

ABA AND CULTURAL DIVERSITY

Lovaas and colleagues (1973) clearly admit that ABA "attempted to teach these children what parents of the middle-class Western world attempt to teach theirs. There are, of course, many questions that one may have about these values, but faced with primitive psychotic children, these seem rather secure and comforting as initial goals" (p. 136). McConnell (2002) recognizes the lack of clarity in ABA-supported programs and he has undertaken a comprehensive examination of the ABA methods in relation to educating students with autism. He argues that most studies done for the purpose of organizing educational programs for autistic persons have focused mainly on ABA materials or scientific information using therapeutic procedures, but none of the activities is adequate for generalization (see Appendixes B and C for examples of what the United Nations says about the rights of the child). The most notable of these experimental procedures are the discrete trial concept or the individualized case studies espoused by Lovaas. Although there is some variability in terms of quality and appropriateness of specific educational interventions, McConnell (2002) has noted, "Experimental investigations can, and most typically do maintain the highest standards of internal validity" Lovaas et al. have expressed the lack of social representation in experimental therapeutic designs but little has been done to expand the cultural diversity in current experimental methods, which are critically important to meeting the needs of a culturally diverse autistic community. Ferster (1961) was the first to apply reinforcers as a behavioural concept in the education of students with autism and he discovered that the absence of reinforcers in educating autistic children accounted for some negative behaviours. He was convinced that with the introduction of reinforcers as a communicative tool autistic children could replace negative behaviours with positive ones and learn new socially accepted skills.

Wolf, Risley, and Mees (1964) were the first behaviourist experts to conduct ABA-using operant condition methods such as behaviour and environmental modifications on a much broader scale. The researchers agree that behavioural education helps autistic children to improve on their verbal skills. Wolf and colleagues (1964) suggested several studies have been undertaken and successful outcomes have been reported by different psychologists, with each one of them claiming that ABA therapy based on shaping environments could help to advance the social, emotional and cognitive independence of people with autism. Thus far, Terrace (1963), Lovaas and Newsom (1976), and Baer and Sherman (1964) have observed that there are several studies that have emerged showing that discriminating learning activities and generalized imitation could have a positive impact on the education of autistic people.

Dempsey and Foreman (2001), and Pratt and associates (2002) have argued that educational intervention programs such ABA are the most practical pedagogical processes for educating autistic students because of their focus on behavioral activities. Tanguay (2000), Baron-Cohen and associates (1992), Gurry and Larkin (1990), Ontario Superior Court of Justice (2005), Gurry and Larkin (1990), and Saegusa (1991) have argued that therapeutic educational interventions in the early life of students with autism could improve autistic students social and cognitive competences and assist them in accessing learning opportunities in special education. However Smith has observed that teachers are making only slight progress because they refuse to develop teaching programs that focus on behavioral problems of the autistic students they teach. Smith (1996) emphasizes that "while many special education programs employ some behavioural procedures, only a small minority can be classified as behaviour analytic" (p. 45). Romanczyk (1996) also makes an interesting observation by alleging that ABA is the most effective solution for assisting autistic students to learn because ABA avoids regimental approaches to teaching. Romanczyk argues that ABA's approach takes into account "a precise and moment-to-moment level of how individuals learn, in the context of their unique physical and social environment, biology, and learning history" (p. 196). However, Lattal and Neef (1996) recent study of reinforcement performance in ABA educational research shows that the ABA process fails to capture the historical roots of target problems and as a result the overall impact of the ABA process on human development is inconclusive and uncertain.

Shea (2004) amplifies the issue of ABA's practicality in special education in her study of Lovaas's work relating to early intensive behavioural intervention for young children with autism. She identified some serious inconsistencies, contradictions and lapses in the ABA concept. Shea observes that "it is time for the professional community to acknowledge to families that although the ABA treatment may be beneficial there is no evidence that it results in 'recovery' or 'normal functioning' in most of its recipients" (p. 363). Shea's observation seems to support the Ontario Ministry of Education's study of the ABA program, which suggests that the contribution of ABA to the educational development of students with autism has not been adequately discussed and as a result the efficacy of therapeutic interventions in helping students with autism to learn remains doubtful (Makin, 2005a, 2005b).

In fact, there is not enough information available to explain how interventionists evaluate the efficacy of interventions they work with when assisting students with autism. Studies have discussed the prescriptive and rigid nature of educational interventions and the difficulty interventionists have in carrying out change. Freire (2003) has observed that "a rigid and oppressive social structure necessarily influences the institutions of child rearing and education within that structure" (p. 154).

Despite the limitations of ABA observed by Tanguay (2000), Baron-Cohen and others (1992), Shea (2004) contends that autism spectrum disorders reveal that when children with autism are exposed to primary intervention programs starting as early as 2 to 3 years of age, autistic children could improve their social and cognitive competences. The revelation has encouraged several studies to emerge over the last decade with different educational intervention concepts resembling a more naturalistic approach. McConnell (2002) observes that flexible and integrative research designs are based on characteristics of social interactions for achieving generalized research outcomes, yet none of the child specific studies derived from ABA could stand on its own.

These primary educational intervention studies have produced a catalogue of social interactive and cognitive skill development activities in group play or classroom-wide settings aimed at offering a viable and practical alternative to ABA's child specific studies. A critical review of literature on educational interventions provides a list of a variety of curricular activities that are specifically designed to increase socialization among children with autism. The list includes: The picture exchange communication system (PECS) (Bondy & Frost, 1994), child choice and preference (Dyer, 1989; Koegel, O'Dell, & Koegel, 1987), time delay (Charlop, Schreibman & Thibodeau, 1985; Halle, 1982), peer interaction (Kennedy & Shukla, 1995), environmental management (Carta, Sainato, & Greenwood, 1988), differential reinforcement (Koegel et al., 1987; Reichle & Sigafoos, 1991), single case intervention (Lovaas, 1977; Baer, Wolf & Risle, 1987; Hersen & Barlow, 1976). These cognitive and socialization techniques are limited because they do not address the diverse cultural and social backgrounds of students' with autism. Besides, they tend to impose the teaching and learning process on the autistic student. For example, child-specific or single case experiments advocated by Lovaas (1977), Baer, Wolf, and Risle (1987), Hersen and Barlow (1976) and differential reinforcement espoused by Koegel and colleagues (1987), and Reichle and Sigafoos (1991).

Since content-based curricular activities allow teachers to decide what should be taught with little consultation with the students, children may have difficulty understanding the material. Kontos, Moore, and Giorgetti (1998) observe that educators better understanding of children's interest and experiences help them to develop inclusive educational activities for improved learning outcomes. For this reason, Kennedy and Shukla (1995) have paid more attention to environmental modification by putting autistic children in groups with typically developing peers or rearranging learning materials to solicit social and cognitive responses. Carta, Sainato and Greenwood (1988) argue on behalf of modification activities by relocating students to different learning environments. Modification experimental designs may have maintained a distinctive advantage over other pedagogic approaches but they are limited in scope and they do not provide adequate information about how to apply the educational design in other cultural domains. Myles and others argue that simply co-locating students is inadequate to produce significant social and cognitive changes in autistic children (Myles, Simpson, Ormsbee, & Erickson, 1993). In addition, Freire (2003) states that "manipulation is another dimension of the theory of anti-dialogical action... by means of manipulation; the dominant elites try to conform the masses to their objectives" (p. 147).

According to the journal entries compiled on Brandon's educational development in March 26, 1995 and April 13, 2005, he had unique social and cognitive abilities that the educational interventions did not represent. Nature and music offered him the tools to communicate his social and intellectual abilities. He found naturally occurring activities and nature based programs reliable because they offered him a place for him to address his interest and learning needs. For Brandon, educational interventions were manipulative and prescriptive pedagogic schemes that offered him no wiggle room to elicit his interest and make possible what he deserved to succeed in school. Brandon's response to educational interventions suggested that he was not comfortable with prescriptive educational activities but preferred to engage in activities that were naturally occurring and nature based.

Brandon comes from a Ghanaian background, which makes him culturally and linguistically different from children of Western countries but curriculum appropriate models for advancing his social and educational skills continue to be available along this socio-cultural frontier. My experience with Brandon's learning indicated that he had unique social and cognitive abilities that were not represented in the educational intervention research literature. For example, the influence of the Ghanaian culture on Brandon's behaviour is strong. Nature and music offered him the tools to communicate his social and intellectual skills. He found naturally occurring activities and nature-based programs reliable because they offered him a place for him to address his interests and learning needs. Brandon's fixation on natural play and lack of interest in PECS and other manipulative educational activities indicated that he was not comfortable with prescriptive pedagogic schemes that offered him no wiggle room for him to follow his interests and develop the knowledge he deserved to succeed in school. Attwood (2008) observes that building on the interest of a child with autism is one of the most important ways for helping the child to learn social skills.

VISUAL COACHING

Handley-Derry's (1997) assessment of Brandon's development indicated that he has a low visual attention level and he had difficulty identifying common objects or pictures. The report recognized that Brandon's attitude to visual schedules and peer mediated interactions were not encouraging relative to training him personal care, social and cognitive skills. It was recommended in the report that Brandon need to improve his visual learning skills. However, Yanchyshyn (1998) had observed in Brandon's initial assessment report for transitional classroom programming that he was a concrete learner who communicates through gestures and movement. Lifshen and Cole's (2002) assessment of Brandon for the Beverley school summer aquatic program recognized that Brandon could work with pictures of objects and he was good in working with picture symbols as a way for recognizing names of his peers on cards.

On the other hand, Boyko (2007) found that Brandon was less interested in visual learning activities. In fact, in working with Brandon, Boyko observed that:

> On one occasion, when presented with pictures of actions which he was required to name, Brandon's first response was to vocalize something unintelligible, then say "no" with frustration, and finally provide the correct action word. At other times, Brandon would begin by saying "Uhhhhhh...," followed by a complete sentence, either in response to what was happening in a picture or a question. Testing of limits on a vocabulary task suggested that Brandon responds well to a fill-in-the-blanks approach (e.g., "It's a _____.") and an exaggerated phonemic prompt, as well as opportunities to look at an adult's face when words, instructions or questions are given. (p. 5)

The visual assessments were important for understanding Brandon's learning needs and how his educational development could be improved. Bondy and Frost (2001) explain the Picture Exchange Communication System (PECS) as "a training system that was developed to teach children with ASD a rapidly acquired, self-initiated functional communication system" (p. 727). PECS has been a professional communicative assessment tool of preference for evaluating autistic students' language and communicative skills. Schwartz and Garfinkle describe PECS as an educational intervention to assist children with functional communication skill deficits. According to Schwartz and Garfinkle (1996), PECS could be applied independently or with spoken language. PECS could broadly be applied in communication development areas such as sign language, electronic and symbol systems. Kravits and associates found that PECS could advance one's functional communication skills and it could also be applied in different learning environments. Kravits, Kamps, Kemmerer, and Potucek (2002) have observed that PECS procedures could be positively taught to improve social and cognitive differences in students with autism to become interactive and communicative developing persons. One of the most important contributions of their study to this research is that the authors observed that PECS's could be applicable retroactively both at home and in the classroom. Brandon's nominal progress with PECS made it possible to look at nature and music as communicative tools for training him to acquire personal care skills.

Demmert (2004) has observed that diagnostic instruments used for assessing the academic performance of students do not present accurate information about the student's abilities. He argues that the standardized assessment tools should not be used universally because students demonstrate significant differences in their social and cognitive competences. Demmert asserts that genetics, experiences and culture influence student performance in school, and that it is imperative that family social backgrounds are adequately understood. Hanson and others (1997) argue that professional assessments often recognize a student's language difficulties, but they refuse to offer a credible solution for a bilingual student with learning difficulties. The authors recognized that most parents become disappointed with the assessment of their children for IEP programming because they feel that the examiners are only interested in promoting English over other languages. Although the American Psychiatry Association (1994) advises professional therapists to be well trained to meet a client's cultural needs before they conduct any examination, the problem is that professionals have difficulty acquiring such important information during their training to improve on their practice. Feltham and Horton (1994) have observed that many professionals have little or no information about their clients, and caution professional examiners not to attend to their work with preconceived ideas about their clients but to engage them productively for the purpose of understanding their creative abilities. Guilt (2007) has problems with contemporary concept of behavioral therapies when he argued in favor of "bridging of the therapy gap' because current therapeutic procedures do no connect with the needs of many minority students.

Brandon's individual education plan (Simmons, 2000) suggested that behavioral therapies have not adequately worked to improve his academic work skills because he is an independent learner who likes to engage in activities that he cared very much about. The report suggested that even with music he would sing songs that he likes and not what others want him to listen to. The report concluded that Brandon's academic work skills improved because he likes to learn about things that were of interest to him. According to the educational plan, Brandon is an independent learner who does well when educational activities are those that meet his needs and appeal to his curiosity. We learn from Brandon's IEP that he is an exceptional student that learns differently from other students and for him to make progress in the classroom, his social and family networks need to be understood by his educator. The IEP informs us that Brandon does not perform well in the classroom in standardized educational programs because he learns differently from typical students.

THE SOCIAL CONSTRUCTION OF ASD

Psychological assessment reports conducted for Brandon's classroom programming revealed the difficulty his examiners confronted whether to approach his learning differences from the clinical or social experience of impairment. In discussing the social construction of ASD, it is important to understand the scholarly debate of Dudley-Marling's (2004) argues that learning disability is socially constructed. According to Dudley-Marling each person has the ability to learn. On the other hand, Marks' (1999) observes that disability is socially constructed for the purpose of segregating some people from becoming equal participants in society. Considering the reviews explains the difficulty Brandon confronted in school because his diagnoses of autism made it difficult for him to have the support that he deserved to have equitable access to education. The social and clinical construction of disability are of particular importance to Brandon's educational development because his experiences in school.

A psychological report completed on Brandon's academic performance in his final year of elementary education (Boyko, 2007), revealed that teachers misconception of autism prevented them from adequately providing the necessary support that Brandon deserved to succeed in school. According to the report the school's lack of understanding of Brandon's interest and needs led him to engage in aggressive behaviour with teaching staff. Earlier psychological assessment reports (Yanchyshyn, 1998; Cole & Lifshen, 1999) had focused primarily on identifying Brandon's classroom needs along clinical interpretations and they overlooked his distinctive capabilities as a way for developing classroom programs that would meet his needs. For example, Yanchyshyn (1998) recommended to "… continue to offer Brandon a program that is structured, consistent and predictable. Whenever possible, pair oral language with visual reinforcement will enhance both expressive and receptive language and will help Brandon attend to activity" (p. 5). The problem with the recommendation was not only its prescriptive nature but the lack of understanding of Brandon's exceptional behaviour. Yanchyshyn failed to consider that Brandon receives and follows instruction in his native language. His lack of spontaneous response to instruction or the difficulty for others to understand his expressive and receptive languages have connection to his use of a second language. The year following, Lifshen and Cole (1999) reported that:

> Brandon was functioning well below the average range on any of the tasks that were presented. He did seem to have some labels for items, could rote count to 13, could match circles and squares and could copy certain lines and a circle. However, it was evident that with his lack of sustained attention and limited skills he would have difficulty in a regular grade one classroom next fall. The results of this psychological assessment indicated that a youngster for whom an intelligence quotient could not reliably be determined at this time. (p. 5)

Lifshen and Cole's lack of understanding of why Brandon demonstrated his lack of interest in classroom activities explained his low performance in the tasks he was tested on. What was interesting in the report was the examiners observation of Brandon's strengths and weaknesses but they were unwilling to exploit his capabilities to improve his overall classroom performance. According to Lifshen and Cole (1999), "Brandon learns when instructions and words are put into a song. Putting information in songs might prove productive to his learning" (p. 4). However, the examiners clinical approach to Brandon's classroom programming was evident because of their reference to the application of "an intelligence quotient" to determine his intellectual abilities. The report revealed the examiners clinical approach to Brandon's classroom planning, which made it difficult for him to have equitable access to education. Boyko (2007) unlike Lifshen and

Cole (1999) takes a constructivist approach to Brandon's classroom programming. Boyko observed that:

> Brandon required a lot of time to process information, and that a variety of prompts were needed to get Brandon to initiate a task, largely due to an apparent lack of understanding. Typically, it took Brandon one trial to understand what was expected on a task, and then he was more likely to initiate responses on his own and persist in completing a task. Brandon's behaviour while completing tasks suggested an inherent sense of mastery and intrinsive motivation to complete tasks presented to him. Also, Brandon was very motivated by social praise in attempting, persisting with, and completing tasks, and in behaving appropriately. (p. 5)

Boyko's observation was important for several reasons. For the first time, it was observed that for one to understand Brandon's classroom behaviour, it is important to identify with his social and learning experiences. The report suggests that Brandon has intellectual capabilities that inform his expressive and receptive languages and to be able to engage him appropriately it is important to understand his social and cognitive skills.

Billington (2006) helps to reconcile the differences between Lifshen and Cole (1999) on one side and Boyko (2007) on the other. Billington (2006) argues that "the models of social deficit often employed to depict autistic children are themselves impaired in their ability to conceptualise individual experience" (p. 2). He argues that there is differences in autism and not disability in autism. Billington's analysis helps to explain Brandon's educational experience in the context of the social versus the clinical construction of autism. Similarly, Shakespeare and Watson have observed that the medical approach does not adequately address the needs of students with impairments. They argue that "the battle for the social model has by no means been won in the world at large, and therefore the main priority is to advocate a social analysis of impairment, not nit-pick or navel-gaze amongst ourselves" (Shakespeare & Watson, 1997, p. 293). According to Shakespeare and Watson, medical sociology refuses to recognize social influences on students with impairments and instead chooses to individualize experiences of people living with developmental impairments. Sinclair (2004) provides a lucid explanation of why social influences on autism cannot be ignored. He argues that typically it takes additional effort to communicate with speakers of different native languages. The needs of the autistic students extend far beyond language and culture, requiring changes in assumptions about shared meanings. This means that people have to make added efforts in their interpretation of autistic students' expressions and make sure that their translations are understood. Sinclair (2004) advises the typical developing world to "give up the certainty that comes of being on your own familiar territory, of knowing you're in charge, and let your child teach you a little of her language, guide you a little way into his world" (p. 1).

Marks' (1999) defence of the social conception of impairment explains that one of the most important aspects of the social conception of impairment is that it recognizes self-advocacy for people with impairment, while the medical approach limits self-sovereignty. According to Marks the life experiences of students with impairments bring to the fore unconscious experiences resident in individual and social experiences. Camilleri (1999) makes a very interesting observation that people are disempowered from impairment labelling. He argues that labelling people as disabled is not the best approach for recognizing developmental differences in people living with impairments. He advocates for an approach that recognizes the social and intellectual contributions of people living with impairments. Camilleri argues against labelling people such as autistic students and emphasizing on their inabilities, instead of their disabilities.

Corker (1999) argues that individual lived experiences or group studies do not adequately capture experiential differences of disabled people for the purpose of conceptualizing differences into social relations. Corker has observed that there will always be differences in what individual experiences offer because experiences happen in particular contexts and at different times, often excluding other experiences. We learn from Gabel and Peters (2004) critique of the social conceptualization of impairment that the social model has been the result of resistance to the medical model relative to the oppression of disabled people. They argue that the social model has also been a premise of oppression against disable people, and the authors observe that resistance theory provides an alternative agency for liberating disabled people from oppression within the medical and social models of impairment.

Danforth's (1999) concept of pragmatism takes an assuaging approach to disabled people's experiences within the social construction of impairment. Danforth claims that democratic dialogue between professionals and parents of disabled persons offers the best approach to understanding the needs of people living with impairments. Danforth (1999), Shakespeare and Watson (2001) identify dialogue as a bridge between medical and social conceptualizations of impairment. The medical and social advances to ASD have informed this study about the variety of approaches to disability education.

EVIDENCE BASED EDUCATION

The Ontario government has introduced a very important special education reform program for helping students with autism spectrum disorders to get access to equitable education in school. For the first time, the government has moved beyond the confine of ABA based educational assessment procedures as a standard for evaluating the skills students with autism bring to the classroom. The evidenced based educational approach has broadened the definition of skills relative to students with autism and how educators should develop these skills to meet the needs of the student. The Minister's Autism Spectrum Disorders Reference Group (2007) and the Ontario Ministry of Education's (2007a) reports define evidence based education as:
    Intensive teaching based on the principles of ABA
- Communication programming that supports the development of spoken language, and may employ visual supports, augmentative communication systems and assistive technology to enable or enhance the development of communication skills

- Strategies to develop and enhance social understanding and skills with structured opportunities for practice in the environment in which the skills are required
- A functional behaviour assessment and analysis
- Modification of curriculum content based on a comprehensive understanding of the student's individual learning profile, and may include alternative approaches to learning.

According to the Ontario government's initiative, the evidence based educational concept would separate curriculum delivery from instructional strategy and offer students with autism the most practical and equitable access to education. However, Prezant and Marshak (2006) offer a different observation by arguing that parents' narrative of experience provides the most important information for the education of children with autism spectrum disorders. We also learn from Horner and associates (2005) that student focused studies offer the most practical evidence for understanding the educational challenges facing students with autism spectrum disorders.

From my experience with Brandon's approach to education, the evidence-based educational strategy would not allow the student to write his or her own story relative to his or her interest in education. Even though, the evidence based approach calls for strategies to develop and enhance information obtained from a student's learning environment, it is difficult for the educator to develop a comprehensive understanding of the information acquired without understanding the socio-cultural character of the environment where the information is obtained. In fact, most student focused studies have been unable to communicate with their readers how students interest in education could be developed and enhanced because of the difficulty in connecting the child's interest to his or her classroom work.

This study advocates for an early identification, development and enhancement of a child's interest in education from birth to adulthood. Such information in my view is the most practical way for empowering both the educator and the student in the classroom. It is understood in this study that students interest change overtime, however, the early identification, development and enhancement of a child's learning interest would not only provide educators a comprehensive understanding of the child's educational needs, it would also prepare educators for meeting future challenges. Such an approach would also address the complex socio-cultural challenges of the child. At present, none of the literature reviewed so far, advocates for such a comprehensive study.

NATURE

Autistic students interactions with nature and music would encourage their experiential learning. Louv's (2006, p. 98) eloquent discussion of "nature deficit disorder and the restorative environment" explains the therapeutic and educational roles nature and nature education play in educating students with impairments. Louv has observed the usefulness of nature as a therapy for students with attention deficit hyperactive disorder (ADHD) and he recommends that parents and educators expose children with impairments to nature experiences. According to Louv nature could replace medications or behavioral therapies by helping students with impairments function productively in society.

Brandon's classroom reports (Ontario Ministry of Education, 2007b) indicated that he was fascinated with zoo animals and nature sites. Teacher reports revealed that whenever Brandon visits the zoo, he demonstrates compassion and a positive interactive spirit towards zoo animals. According to his teachers, Brandon has a sense of empathy for animals and his zoo behaviour demonstrates his passion, belief and value system for animal life. We also learn from the reports that Brandon has developed a positive understanding of zoo animals and he likes to interact with them. In my journal entry for June 20, 2006, I wrote down the following observation:

> Our visit to the Toronto Public Zoo has been a very educative event for both Brandon and me. He has been pointing to different species of birds with different beaks, wings, tails and feet. He is showing deep interest in birds such as the bald eagle, black-necked stilt, black oystercatcher, brown pelican, and the pileated woodpecker because of the different colours, shape and sizes of the beaks of the birds.

Tarski (2007) has observed that children learn from interacting with birds. Introducing children to birds, tree-planting and playing in the bushes near bird sanctuaries could help children learn about the ecology of birds. Taski claims, "As the kids notice the bird building a nest or singing good-night, offer a fact or two that would make sense for their age group. But let them enjoy and absorb the wonder without a lecture" (p. 1). Tarski asserts that such interacting with birds could connect students to their natural settings as well as help them learn more about the world around them. Gibbons (2008) has also observed that the interaction with birds could introduce people to progressive ideas and new information about themselves, their relationship with others and the natural world.

Since nature and natural occurrences are cross-cultural they could promote a cultural dialogue as well as connect home-based learning with classroom practice. Bizerril (2004) reminds the study to explore problem-solving ideas beyond one's own experience to encompass other real life experiences capable of transforming learning experiences of students with autism. Lukas and Ross (2005) have observed that zoo and aquatic animals have important influences on how children learn and behave. The authors argue that zoo and aquatic species could empower children to develop problem-solving skills to advance their school performance. Smith-Sebasto and Semrau (2004) have observed that children interacting with birds and other animal species could teach them how to develop positive attitudes, resilience and self-confidence because they learn from these species how they develop attitudes, beliefs, values and toughness to overcome adversity in their own habitat.

Gough (1997) and Wheeler and Bijur (2000) refer to nature education as the awareness of the natural environment. Gough argues that nature education is about the strengthening of human relationship and commitment to a healthy planet. Wheeler and Bijur agree that nature education is about developing positive nature values and practices.

NAMING OF ANIMALS

In most nature literature, exotic naming has been a common practice that has had far-reaching consequences on children's understanding of themselves, relationships to others and their place in the natural world. The existing pedagogic disconnection between children and nature has prevented many children from fully understanding the natural world. Such educational neglect is consistent with Shepard's observation that humans misunderstanding of nature are driven by inadequate information, flawed techniques and insensibility (Shepard, 1982). Louv also informs us that "lacking direct experience with nature, children begin to associate it with fear and apocalypse, not joy and wonder" (2008, p. 134). Shepard and Louv share a similar idea about nature that it has a positive impact on human behaviour. Wells (2000) makes a similar observation when she said, "the effects of natural elements within the home environment have a profound effect on children's cognitive functioning" (p. 790).

Nature is a natural creation that connects people to their natural environment, and it is the home of every culture irrespective of the geographical location. Nature transcends culture and nature is what gives meaning to human life. The naming of nature by one group against the other limits one's intellectual and moral freedom (Dewey, 1997). Contemporary nature education has mostly been about adults' perceptions and actions. Nature educators must move beyond conceptual and theoretical arguments to everyday natural occurrences and practices. Several studies have argued that contemporary nature literature does not adequately address the social and cultural needs of children because children find it difficult to connect the information they obtain from nature texts to their everyday nature experiences.

MUSIC

Brandon's initial psychological assessment and classroom reports indicated his deep interest in music and how music helped him to learn. Yanchyshyn (1998) observed that at age 5 Brandon liked listening to music and he could sing words of familiar songs without any help. Thomas (2001) noted that Brandon is enthusiastic about listening to music. He demonstrates an excellent memory for music, classroom poetry and familiar books. Ansley (2003) reported that Brandon expresses an insatiable interest for music and he prefers listening to music whenever he has a break from classroom activities. Ansley has observed that music helps Brandon to improve his classroom behaviour. According to Ansley, he does not participate in the classroom "sing song sessions," but he is able to sit and listen to music for a sustained period of time. Smits (2003, p. 4) writes "Brandon participated in the ORFF music program this term. In this program he manipulated the basic elements of music such as dynamics (volume), and tempo (fast, slow). He created rhythmic patterns using a variety of sounds (bells, drums, clapping, stomping). Excellent participation this term! Great job Brandon!" Brandon's teachers inform this study about the role music has played in Brandon's academic development. This was an important development for a child with autism who had been identified by his family physician and psychological expert as having social, language and cognitive deficits (Handley-Derry, 1997; Li, 2007).

The Ontario Ministry of Education and Training (1998) states that by the time students' complete grade one, they should be able to demonstrate competence in basic elements of music to be able to listen, perform and create music. The school expects students to develop appropriate vocabulary and musical proficiency across cultures. But we learn from Van Berckelaer-Onnes (2003) there are no longitudinal studies available to show how children acquire music competence. This brings me to the question: what could teachers do to help autistic students achieve music and free musical play skills to improve their social and cognitive skills? Smithrim (1997) has observed that children early engagement in free musical play activities contribute to growth in music competence. Littleton (1991) study about children exposure to musical play demonstrated that free musical play offered children opportunities to listen, improvise and create music on their own. Taggart (2000) has observed exposing children to free musical play activities helps them to be creative in academic work. Neelly (2001) argues that "children respond naturally to music, lyrics, rhythms and positive social interactions during musical play" (p. 34). Mathews' (2000) found that there is no such activity as non-musical when it comes to children's free musical learning.

Although, we learned from Neelly (2001) and Van Berckelaer-Onnes (2003) and Ungerer and Sigman (1981) that autistic students could also develop their free play musical skills with the appropriate support, Brandon's social, language and cognitive problems offered me, his teachers and many behavioural experts that worked with him little hope. However, he demonstrated his resilience and self-confidence by using music to overcome his developmental difficulties. For example, we learn from Brandon's teachers that he improved his social and cognitive skills with his interest in music.

EDUCATIONAL DEVELOPMENT

The Organization for Economic Co-operation and Development (OECD, 2000) provides a definition and description of students with special needs and discusses issues with special needs education. The study identifies special needs students as coming from three cultural domains, namely: students with physical impairments and impairments that affect learning, students with learning handicaps not connected with impairments, and students with learning difficulties associated with socio-economic, cultural and linguistic factors. According to the OECD the definition, description and identification of "special needs" varies depending on the country, and international comparisons help to understand descriptive variations across cultures and how differences influence education delivery. Recognizing cultural differences is important for organizing education programs and services for autistic students. Wilder and colleagues (2004) bring professional attention to cultural differences between autistic symptoms and culturally appropriate behaviours. The authors argue that differences exist regarding how autistic students access special education programs and services across cultures. Dyches and associates (2004) have observed that most researchers and practitioners ignore race and other multicultural issues in autism research. The authors argue that the oversight has undermined efforts to generalize autism research outcomes.

Similarly, Demmert (2004) asserts that culture influences a student's view of the world and how the student would approach a problem. He argues that culture is not static but evolves over time, and that the influences of culture on a student's social and cognitive development should be taken into account in any organized pedagogic environment. Hanson, Gutierrez, Brennan, and Zercher (1997) argue that culture influences how a student socializes with peers and that socialization is the key to higher achievement in school. The authors argue that students' interests in education transcend cultural barriers in school. Elder and colleagues observed that autistic persons have difficulty in initiating appropriate communication with others, but with the appropriate support at home these children could improve on their social and academic work skills. According to Gabel (2002), one of the most important gaps in education is that teachers refuse to recognize the ability diversity in disable children in school. In order for schools to achieve progress in the classroom, they should organize classroom activities such that students' individual abilities are recognized and engaged creatively.

A STUDY OF A LIVED EXPERIENCE

Max Van Manen (1990) describes phenomenological research as a search for what it means to be human. In essence, phenomenology is a means to understand the human experience. We also learn from Glesne (1999) that a phenomenological study focuses on descriptions of how people experience real life situations and how they learn from their experiences of the phenomena under study. For Cashin (2003) phenomenology provides a framework for exploring the experiences of parents with children with autism spectrum disorders by learning from their experiences in a genuine conversation that could not have been possible to obtain from reading text. We learn from Reid (1999) that learning from the experiences of families with children with autism spectrum disorders provide important information for understanding the experiences of children with autism.

The Ministers' Autism Spectrum Disorders Reference Group (2007) has recognized that learning from the experiences of students with autism spectrum disorders offer important ways for developing conversational relationships with them. The Ontario Ministry of Education (2007b) advises educators to acquire information from their daily experiences with students with autism spectrum disorders because they offer educational opportunities for the development of activities that are appropriate for meeting each students needs.

One of the most important aspects of this phenomenological study is the narrative character of the lived experience under study. According to Cashin (2003) through narrative of experience we come to understand parents' experiences with autism spectrum disorders in a distinctive way. Connelly and Clandinin (1988) inform us that "When we think of life as a whole, we tend to think narratively. We tell stories about ourselves that are historical, explanatory, and foretelling of the future" (p. 24). Narrative inquiry offers a conceptual, an empirical and a methodological approach to reflectively reconstruct past experiences to help us understand our lives and plan for the future. Dewey (1916; 1938), Connelly and Clandinin (1988; 1990) contend that the study of experience reminds us to think of life as a whole because human experiences are educative when it is connected with other life experiences. According to the literature study phenomenology helps Brandon and I to understand the meaning of our lives and the narrative character of our experiences connects us with the human experience. The narrative quality of our experience allows the study to tell a family's experience and to relive the experience such that others may learn from the experience. Crites (1971) observes that a narrative study brings a story to a full meaning because stories are rooted in experience.

Sacks' (1985) observes that narrative helps us to reflect on our experiences, our inner feelings, and what we can become. We learn from Connelly and Clandinin (1988, p. 24) that narrative study is "the study of how humans make meaning of experience by endless telling and retelling stories about themselves that both refigure the past and create purpose in the future." I anticipate that by discussing these conceptual frameworks and reflecting on my own life stories, I would be able to learn from my experience and tell my story in a way that would help me to understand my parent/educator experience in the field of contemporary education. Dewey, Connelly and Clandinin's ideas of education place educational value on my experience with Brandon's learning because they argue that experience is educational.

One of the most important aspects of this study is the role phenomenological narrative studies play in my story. The phenomenological and narrative characters of the study have allowed me to make meaning of my experience. By studying my experience with Brandon, I have come to understand the role of father research in this study. Reid (2008) argues that father research addresses a significant gap in knowledge by providing authentic information about how fathers, in the context of the family, influence child development. Father research makes it possible to learn about a father's experience in child rearing. Fabiano (2007) has observed that research on parenting has generally focused on mothers, with a father's parenting participation marginally explored. According to Fabiano (2007) "parents who are consistent, self-confident, and affectionate raise socially competent children" (p. 683). He argues that active parenting produces socially competent children and inactive parenting brings into being poorly prepared children for a socially competitive world.

Journal entries compiled on Brandon's development suggest that (Osei, 2008), he was a socially interactive child who enjoys outdoor activities such as bird watching with his parents and siblings. Brandon's interest in outdoor play and music has helped him to make important progress in school. The journal record reveals that active parenting has helped Brandon to develop self-confidence, academic achievement, and stability in peer relationships. It was also observed that my experience with Brandon's learning skills motivated me to conduct this father research.

Thomas, Krampe, and Newton (2008) have observed that active parenting helps children to develop socialization and productive academic work skills. Boyko (2007) has also observed that Brandon's exposure to behavioral assessments has made those working with him to understand him better and has contributed positively to improving his classroom programming. The journal record also indicates that when Brandon was diagnosed with autism in 1997, he was exposed to a variety of therapeutic procedures to support his social and academic work.

Although, the behavioral assessments have made an important contribution to Brandon's social and intellectual development, it was Brandon's interest in birds and birdsongs and a father's narrative of experience in nature and nature education that provided a much needed support for coaching him to develop personal care skills. For example, it was his interest in birds and birdsongs that advanced his interest in developing toileting skills.

PARENT ADVOCACY

Over the last decade, families have used the courts to demand improvements in educational programs and services for autistic students in special education programs. In response the courts have recommended additional funding as a way to address the current impasse in special education for autistic students. The issue here is whether autistic students would benefit from therapeutic treatment packages based on ABA principles. Studies have suggested that autism and autism-related behaviours should not be subjected to professional services or therapeutic treatments alone. Billington (2006), Sinclair (2004), Moore (2000) and Ryan (1995) have asserted that educators should search for imaginative ways of understanding and dialoguing with the autistic student. More recently authors such as Grandin (2001), Sinclair (2004), and Willey (1999) have begun to write about their lived experiences with autism and the difficulty the typical developing world has in developing communication with people living with autism. The authors have suggested that educators (teachers, parents and professional service providers) develop creative and productive ways for dialoguing with people living with autism.

Studies have suggested that developing learning relationship with autistic students is the most practical way for understanding their learning needs, but available evidence suggests that many educators do not have the experience and information needed to communicate effectively with children with autism. Billington (2006) argues for problem-solving ways for engaging autistic students as a means to understanding their educational needs. His concept of engagement opposes the orthodoxy of prescriptive education (see Appendix D for additional information relative to the role of parental advocacy in the education of children with autism spectrum disorders). Billington advises educators that prescriptive engagement with autistic students make it impossible for their educational needs to be understood. In a similar discussion, Hodge (2007) recounts that the diagnostic approach to ASD has undermined parent and child relationship in the sense that professional treatment packages do not reflect parental experience of their children and the parenting skills parents have developed as primary educators. The problem has also affected parental influence on the organization of their children's classroom work.

Studies about autistic students social and cognitive needs have identified dialogue as the best possible way for cultivating the academic interest of students with autism. Hodge has observed that many parents caring for their autistic children have experienced difficulty developing a comprehensive dialogue with professional service providers because these experts come with ready-made solutions that force parents to accept the diagnostic stigmatization of their children. The examiner identifies professional stigmatization and hegemonic use of power as some of the difficult experiences autistic students face in education. Hodge argues that autistic students oppressive conditions articulate the need for a new educational praxis founded on equity and social justice.

Early studies have been very critical of the way researchers and educators have identified and classified social and cognitive differences in autistic students and the need to develop learning relationships with autistic students. Billington has observed that most researchers and educators erroneously use terms such as "social deficits" to describe that autistic students are impaired in their ability to express themselves freely and that has negatively impacted the way they are taught in schools. On the same note, Goode (2007) argues that researchers and practitioners often treat students' self-expressions as a contingent and temporal experience to rationalize the subjugation of disabled students to "externally-imposed constraints" on the parameters for negotiation. For many autistic students, dialogue has been denied for far too long and Freire's idea of dialogue offers them the best hope for finding their place in pedagogy.

Furthermore, studies have discussed at length the marginalization of autistic students diverse abilities from pedagogic inception to classroom delivery, coupled with the fact that ABA techniques continue to inform classroom planning and delivery for many autistic students in education. Hence, it is important that through this study, one student's knowledge of nature as objective reality is explored to adequately inform the special education field. Brandon's consciousness of nature and its relationship to his willingness to learn, which developed from his own real experiences, might help to address some of gaps in information in the organization of special education programs for autistic students across diverse learning communities.

SUMMARY

In summary, developing effective communication with Brandon has come about from his own interest in nature and music and the experience of a father who saw the opportunity to expand Brandon's experience into new areas. The gap in information relative to ASD and the organization of special education for autistic students reflects how a family's experience with autism and a way of living with the experience in public education. The literature study has focused on how Brandon has used his interest in birds and birdsongs to address the gap in knowledge of his experience of education.

The province of Ontario's Education Act 1990 R.S.O. encourages parents to be the primary advocates for their children and it also allows parents to participate in the decision-making process. The special education guidelines provide information about how teachers and parents should work together for the benefit of the student, and this means parents could hold schools accountable to what they find inappropriate. However, studies show that there is not a well-defined process or information to prepare parents to make informed decisions on behalf of their children. Baker (1989) has observed that parents' lack of information has generated to a lack of interest in the planning and implementation of education for their autistic children because few parents have the requisite information to contribute positively to the planning and delivery process.

The literature study has helped me to improve my fathering practice by providing me the information I needed to work progressively with Brandon. I also observed in this study that the literature review informed me in extraordinary ways by helping me to understand the social and cognitive needs of children living with autism spectrum disorders. Brandon's interest in nature and music has made it easy for me and his teachers to work with him. For example, Brandon's parents and teachers participated in several IEP meetings and other educational planning activities that allowed us to discuss the educational opportunities in nature and music learning.

A METHODOLOGICAL FRAMEWORK

We might say that hermeneutic phenomenology is a philosophy of the personal, the individual, which we pursue against the background of an understanding of the evasive character of the logos of the other, the whole, the communal, or the social. Much of educational research tends to pulverize life into minute abstracted fragments and particles that are of little use to practitioners. So it is perhaps not surprising that a human science that tries to avoid this fragmentation would be gaining more attention. (Van Manen, 1990, p. 7)

This study represents a family's collaborative learning experience with a 14-year old autistic student (Brandon), who in his early life has developed an interest in nature and music as communicative tools for his educational transformation. Brandon's emotional interactions with birds and birdsongs and his fascination with fruit gardens encouraged us as a family to follow with keen interest his curiosity in nature. Over the past 14 years, as a family we have observed and documented phenomenological events and situations in our interactions with Brandon and his quest to explore the natural environment as a means for advancing his academic work skills. Our interactions with Brandon have included a reflection and documentation of our experiences, and developing creative ideas from what we have learned together to improve our relationship. In an effort to understand Brandon's primary experiences with birds and birdsongs, I reflected on my own childhood nature experiences and I found what Van Manen (1990) describes as "theory of the unique" (p. 156).

The theory of the unique is reflective of Brandon's interests in birds and birdsongs that are not represented in text. I have also realized the unique educational qualities in nature and music that have influenced Brandon to develop an understanding of himself, his relationship with others and his place in the natural world. By collaborating on our experiences, we make meaning of our lives and in the process empower each other to act consciously with others and the world. This data gathering identifies the unique character of children's experiences and the need to develop a concerted effort for understanding the everyday experiences of children. We are also reminded of Freire's (2003) notion that "Consequently, no one can say a true word alone-nor can she say it for another, in a prescriptive act which robs others of their words" (p. 88). Van Manen notes that parenting is more than theorizing issues because it involves making constant choices and intentional decision making. The data gathered in the present study reflected the constant choices and intentional decisions that have been made over the years with my interactions with Brandon. Van Manen (1990) attempts to convince us that:

Human science research produces theory of the unique. And it is a feature of theory of the unique that it appropriates the particular case, and not prospectively or introspectively, but retrospectively. Our living with children in natural situations of parenting and teaching is much less characterized by constant choice and rational decision making than theories of the teacher as "reflective practitioner" and "deliberative decision maker" have made us to believe. (p. 156)

The term phenomenological research identifies the broad domain of research approaches in the experience of education. Even though phenomenological study and human science narrative represent different epistemological interests, both are located in lived experience in the human experience. The study is developed as hermeneutic phenomenology, a human science with a focus on the study of persons. Phenomenology is the descriptive reporting of how one learns about the lived experiences of everyday life and hermeneutics explains how the experience is interpreted into text. Hermeneutic phenomenology relates well with the experience of fathering autism. I expect that through a phenomenological inquiry into Brandon's life over the last 14 years, I will come to understand my lived experience with autism and how the experience has influenced my life.

The phenomenological study has captured our lived experiences with Brandon in a way that has helped us to understand his social and academic work skills. It is also about my own search for fathering identity in terms of where I have been, who I am and where I might go in my educational experience of parenting and caring for one autistic child. The phenomenological discovery of the self through one's lived experience is consistent with Freire's (2003) conception that "for the truly humanist educator and authentic revolutionary, the object of action is the reality to be transformed by them together with other people-not other men and women them- selves" (p. 94). Here we learn from Freire that making Brandon an active participant in the study not only helps us to learn with him but it advances knowledge. This is also true of Noddings' notion of caring (Noddings, 1984).

In our stories and through phenomenological experiences, we come to understand our ways of being and caring as we make meaning of how we experience the world. Phenomenology of personal experience has a universal appeal because it helps us to understand the self in relationship with others and the world. We learn from Casey (1996) that phenomenology of a storied life helps one to understand lived experience relative to others and one's place in the world.

THE NARRATIVE CHARACTER OF THE STUDY

Brandon's nature and music stories revealed interesting information and extraordinary connections to my own storied life as a child growing up in a rich natural environment. Although the places and the times where our experiences occurred reflect socio- cultural and generational differences, the educational and experiential contents in our stories are similar. Our interests in birds and fascination with fruit gardens married us to nature and in the process gave our storied lives their meanings. Through my narrative quality of experience I have come to understand my storied life with Brandon in the praxis of education (Freire, 1985). Freire talks about conscientization as emerging from isolation into inclusion with a level of consciousness that is self- empowering, liberating and propelling subjects onto future productive experiences.

Freire's notion of conscientization is consistent with learning through nature and nature education for improving knowledge of self, relationship with others and the world. Relative to autism, our learning about nature and nature education has empowered us to pursue our collective interest in birds, dolphins, fruit gardens, and nature play. In a sense, we have developed a dialogic relationship with each other in a way that has made it easier for us to deal with autism. The experience has helped us to regain self-consciousness that allows our social orderings to relate to the beliefs we hold about nature. In retrospect, the search for a meaning in our storied lives has brought us to a reflective quality of experience and its affinity with nature. Reflecting on our storied lives constitutes a major part of the data collected to develop this study.

FATHER RESEARCH AS A PHENOMENON

One of the phenomena considered in this study is the role a father plays in the educational development of his autistic child. As the genre of father-research suggests, the principal focus of a father researcher is the study of his children (Reid, 2008). Although this study focuses on the experiences of a child, it also reveals the experiences of a father and a son, the researcher and the phenomena; it is an inquiry into the interpersonal relationship. Father research involves caring for children, raising them, reflecting and learning from the experience. The notion of father research is consistent with Van Manen's observation that "Pedagogy is the activity of teaching, parenting, educating, or generally living with children, that require constant practical acting in concrete situations and relations" (Van Manen, 1990, p. 2). According to Van Manen, hermeneutic phenomenology involves being conscious in knowing the self and how it relates to others and the world.

Father research fits well into the phenomenological study of father and child experience and making sense out of the experience, which is consistent with Freire's relational pedagogy that is a way of connecting the self with others and the world. Freire claims that "only men, as "open" beings, are able to achieve the complex operation of simultaneously transforming the world by their action and grasping and expressing the world's reality in their creative language" (Freire, 1985, p. 68). This view is shared in Dewey's discussion of the relationship between "seeming" and "being" (Dewey, 1938). Dewey contends that knowing is doing and without knowing there is no doing. My role as a researcher is to learn about my life, its relationship to others and my place in the world.

WHAT IS FATHER RESEARCH?

Until the 1970's, research concerning fathering and the father's roles in the family was sparse. Parenting research emphasized the mother and her importance within the family. In recent years, the father's recognition as an integral and vital member of the child-rearing team has emerged, although the amount of research regarding the father and fathering remains small in comparison with the subject of mothers. (Boyd, 1985, p. 112).

45

The term "father research" has been used by several researchers to describe fathers' experiences of their children and the desire to think, reflect, write and develop the experiences to text. Father research contributes significant knowledge to how fathers and mothers, in families, influence their children's development. In my literature review I did not come across this term being used to study a father's experience with his autistic child's development. Research approaches on parenting have usually focused on mothers, with father parenting approaches relatively less studied. Fabiano's (2007) recent study on father parenting has revealed that the majority of research studies on parenting have focused on mothers as researchers or participants. Little or no emphasis has been given to father-related studies.

There have been father researchers who have studied their own children's development but these studies are limited and they have not provided adequate information needed to address the challenges in early childhood education. For example, Darwin (1877) and Sidebotham's (2002) extraordinary works with their children's development have provided valuable insights into social and scientific studies. Darwin (1877) work responded to Taine's (1877) study on the acquisition of language with "a biographical sketch of an infant," and the information he had collected over a thirty- year period prior to his own son's development helped to inform education research (Darwin, Taine, as cited in Crystal, no date, p. 78). Darwin's data was previously used to develop his larger 1872 work, "The Expression of the Emotions in Man and Animals." In recent years, Sidebotham's (2002) work on "The Doctor, the Father, and the Social Scientist" has demonstrated how a father researcher's reflection on his own child's development helped advance paediatrics studies. Sidebotham's study of parent/child relationships in paediatrics was an effort to improve paediatrics professional practice. One of the most important contributions Sidebotham's studies has made to medical science is in showing what influence father research might have on a paediatrician's practice. We learn from the study that paediatricians can draw information from their parenting practice to improve their professional practice.

WHY A FATHER IN FATHER RESEARCH?

Although this study is firmly rooted in the phenomenological research in the social science domain, its relational importance to father research and a father's experience in caring, raising, educating and learning with his son should not be under-emphasized. Father research provides fathers the tools to present their stories in authentic ways that no other research method can match. The Federal Interagency Forum on Child and Family Statistics (1998) has observed that "Research on father-hood has been hampered by a lack of data about men and directly from men. Much less is known about becoming and being a father than is known about becoming and being a mother" (p. 1). Bronte-Tinkew and Moore (2004) have also observed that a father is the better prepared researcher to provide accurate and bona fide information about his experience with his child than what others might write on his behalf. As a father who wants to share his story, father research provides me the opportunity to advance my intellectual growth by reconstructing my own story. This is the best way to help inform others.

THE RESEARCH PARTICIPANT

Brandon is severely limited in language and social skills. Although it is difficult for him to understand most people, I have been his primary caretaker and communicator and we have learned to understand each other. I have recently made great strides in helping him to understand what autism is. Over the years, he has learned to say words and has developed language skills but his limited use of language has made it difficult for him to communicate with others. Our dialogic interactions in the past 14 years have given Brandon and me a communication with each other that is quite special. Brandon's interest, actions and words are the focus of the data collected for developing this study. The data has been collected throughout Brandon's life. I have been recording notes, taking pictures, collecting artefacts (drawings and musical library), school reports, health information—the stuff that all parents collect as part of the process of archiving growth and development. My journals about my parenting were started long before I decided that this would be my thesis. My wife Doris has been helpful in explaining to Brandon his role in my thesis research (see Appendix A for an example of a letter asking Doris to explain the research process to Brandon).

I have over the years shared with him my notes and journals and he enjoys hearing stories about himself. I will read him stories, the narratives that are my data, and ask him if it is alright for other people to read the stories about him. He is the star of the movie, the main character in the story, the hero. It is a story about Brandon and his family. It is a story that will help others, and he is a part of it. Brandon was reminded about how much he loves nature and music and the importance of communicating his experience in my study. I shared with Brandon the experiences we have shared over the years. For example, the nature trips we have taken together over the years and the pictures that we have taken were activities that reminded him about our nature experiences. I also showed him home made videos about the nature activities that we have enjoyed together to help him recollect his thoughts on the things that have influenced his educational development. I have read to Brandon the notes that I have written on our nature experiences, begun when he was three months old, to inform him about where we have been and where we might go.

METHODOLOGY AND DESIGN

This research project took place in a collaborative family environment and attempts to describe and report on my experience of fathering autism: I have interpreted the data and my experiences into text (Van Manen, 1990). The study was developed into three main data acquisition clusters: storytelling, outdoor activities and reading exercises. This was to allow Brandon to participate fully in the study. The nature talk exercise provided Brandon and me the opportunity to speak directly to each other and to address any concerns either one of us had. The outdoor activities were designed to offer Brandon and me the opportunity to participate in nature trips and engage in organized play activities for the purpose of learning about nature. Finally, reading to Brandon also helped us to communicate our experiences freely with each other and allow Brandon to authenticate or correct stories he agreed or disagreed with.

CONVERSATION

One of the most important sources of gathering data for developing this study was from conversations Brandon and I had about nature and music. We talked and asked questions about our connections to nature and music, and the role nature and music has played in Brandon's education. We discussed several nature issues such as why birds mimic sounds or why many birds have beaks in different shapes, sizes and colours. We also discussed what sounds would be appropriate to mimic with birds. Our discussions helped us to focus our attention on our individual and social issues that we wanted to know more about. We developed conversations and social stories into songs and we sang to each other as a way for addressing our frustrations in our lives as well as looking forward to a productive future.

Developing conversations with Brandon encouraged him to share with me issues that were on his mind. On several occasions, we talked about why migratory birds and why they travel from place to place. Whenever, he would look at me with a smile, I knew that he understood what we were discussing. Whenever he stares at me, I knew he had a question. I would then use probing questions like "Are you okay Brandon?" or "What is wrong?" to get more information from him to answer the question on his mind. Brandon would answer either "no" or "okay." Such interactions were helpful in helping me to help him.

At times, I sang to him and he would ask me to sing to him again. After I have sang to him repeatedly (two or three times), I would ask Brandon to share with me what he likes and dislikes about my song. His answers usually provided me the opportunity to follow up with probing questions that would usually lead to new information about his learning needs and expectations. Another important aspect of singing to Brandon was to assure him that Daddy loves him and to encourage him to share with me issues that may have been preoccupying him at the particular instance. Brandon's utterances and ideas helped me to develop fluid conversations with him and the experiences have been audio taped and transcribed to help me develop the main arguments in the study. I also videotaped and transcribed Brandon's interactions with birds on the park because whenever he was in the presence of birds and birdsongs he fashioned impulses, facial expressions and utterances that were interesting and very much connected to issues in his mind. For example, a particular yelp of a bird would remind him of a rhythm in one of his favourite songs and that would motivate him to sing or share a story about a song on his mind with me. These revelations have been developed as a part of the study.

THE OUTDOOR TRIPS

One of the most important sources of gathering data for developing this study was from conversations Brandon and I had about nature and music. We talked and asked questions about our connections to nature and music, and the role nature and music has played in Brandon's education. We discussed several nature issues such as why birds mimic sounds or why many birds have beaks in different shapes, sizes and colours. We also discussed what bird sounds would be appropriate to mimic. Our discussions helped us to focus our attention on the individual and social issues that we wanted to know more about. We developed conversations and social stories into songs and we sang to each other as a way to address the frustrations in our lives and look forward to a productive future.

Talking with Brandon encouraged him to share with me issues that were on his mind. On several occasions, we talked about why birds migrated. Whenever he would look at me with a smile, I knew that he understood what we were discussing. Whenever he stared at me, I knew he had a question. I would then use probing questions like "Are you okay Brandon?" or "What is wrong?" to get more information from him so as to help answer the question on his mind. Brandon would answer either "no" or "okay." Such interactions were helpful in helping me to help him.

At times, I sang to him and he would ask me to sing to him again. After I had sung to him repeatedly (two or three times), I would ask him to share with me what he liked and disliked about my song. His answers usually provided me the opportunity to follow up with questions that would usually lead to new information about his learning needs and expectations. Another important aspect of singing to Brandon was to assure him that Daddy loves him and to encourage him to share with me issues that may have been preoccupying him at the particular instance. Brandon's utterances and ideas helped me to develop fluid conversations with him; the experiences were audio taped and transcribed to help me develop the main arguments in the study. I also videotaped and transcribed Brandon's interactions with birds in the park because whenever he was in the presence of birds and birdsongs he fashioned impulses, facial expressions and utterances that were interesting and very much connected to issues in his mind. For example, a particular yelp of a bird would remind him of a rhythm in one of his favourite songs and that would motivate him to sing or share a story about a song on his mind with me. These revelations have been developed as a part of the study.

READING EXERCISES

Reading to Brandon was one of the most remarkable experiences a father could have with his autistic son in naturalistic settings. The reading exercises helped us to communicate our experiences as well as allowing Brandon to direct his interests as he desired. He would point to a bird and he expected me to tell him the name of that bird. After I had answered his question he would use the information to communicate with that particular bird. The learning behaviour was unusual. I observed that reading to Brandon encouraged him to communicate with me his needs and expectations. Reading also motivated Brandon to read back to me and to participate in activities that were of interest to him. Reading nature books helped me to learn for the first time his insatiable interest in dolphins.

His actions encouraged us to develop functional communication around the bio-physical activities of marine animals such as dolphins.

CHALLENGES IN DATA COLLECTION

Although storytelling, outdoor activities and reading exercises offered the most fluid way for communicating with Brandon and addressing his needs during the data gathering process, the data collection method was nonetheless faced with serious challenges. There were times when Brandon did not show any interest hearing the songs I sang to him, or books I read to him, and at times he would show no interest in leaving the house. These behavioural changes presented significant challenges that required critical decision-making as to what to do. I would modify the environment by reading one of his favourite books to him or introduce him to an outdoor activity that I thought would appeal to his interest. On several occasions, when he had had a difficult day at school he would show his unwillingness to communicate with me. In such instances, none of the data collection techniques would work with him and I would have to persuade him with a candy or his favourite strawberry ice cream to get him to speak with me. The winter months were difficult to go on outdoor trips and collect data. What we did in the winter was to spend time listening to music.

TOOLS AND FIELD TEXTS

The study used multifaceted and multidimensional approaches in data gathering to describe and interpret the lived experiences of the subject. The tools for data collection have been audiotapes of conversations, videotapes of social and learning activities, school reports, family pictures, books and Brandon's intimate interactions with birds and fruit gardens. Many of our conversations with Brandon and his spontaneous utterances were audio taped and they have been developed as part of the study. There were video recordings of social and family events that have been transcribed and the information added to the study. Information from Brandon's school reports was used to develop key areas of the study. Information from family pictures that told relevant stories about our experiences with Brandon as well as our intimate interactions with him before and after he was diagnosed with autism invoked important memories and the information developed was introduced to the study.

Several tools were employed in a variety of ways to increase the authenticity and clarity of the data collected (Glesne, 1999). For example, songbirds and acrobatic dolphins were employed as pedagogical tools for teaching Brandon how to acquire language and use words. The experience of teaching Brandon words using the physiology of songbirds and acrobatic dolphins were recorded as primary data and the information has been used to develop the study. Relative to gathering information on Brandon's school performance, several reports were used to provide data and information; Brandon's IPRC and IEP reports provided valuable information about exploring home training activities as well as his classroom work. In addition to my personal observation of his classroom development, teacher assignments were used to develop the study.

There were several scholarly texts that inspired and enlightened me as I searched for ways of reflecting, reporting and converting my story to text. Margo Tupper's (1966) literary work No Place to Play has contributed immensely to the organization of this study. Richard Louv's (2006) Last Child in the Woods has helped me to re-connect with my past nature experiences that I may have taken for granted. In both texts, the authors shared their childhood stories with their children about the nature play places they enjoyed when they were children. Nature places have been a part of my nature identity. I found out that the data collected to develop the study is inadequate unless it recognizes Brandon's experiences of nature play places and what they have meant to our experience with autism.

The documentary research was an opportunity to delve into the culture of journal writing, the places where I have been, events and situations in my life, who I am and where I want to go. The journal records covered my early childhood nature learning on the farm, the many years of playing in natural environments and built landscapes and my experience of fathering autism. I conducted a regular review of journal entries detailing Brandon's development in the first 15 months of life before he was formally diagnosed with a developmental disorder. The second part of the journal writing focused on Brandon's development after the formal diagnosis of (GDD/PDD), from the fifteenth month of life to the present. This includes his early outdoor activities and school and psychological reports. Naturally, the journal account also has been a personal journey of discovering the self as well as coming to terms with the successes and disappointments in my personal life. Collecting publications on autism, as well as artefacts and photographs, has been a very productive educational and therapeutic exercise for me over the past decade. The documentary records have helped me to reflect on experiences from my early childhood to fatherhood. The lived experiences in a way have connected my past experiences with the future. The documentary review and reflection have also helped the study to develop structure and to focus on important experiences that stand out in my interactions with Brandon.

METHODS OF DATA ANALYSIS AND PRESENTATION

This dissertation is developed into three thematic clusters for the purpose of data collection, analysis and presentation. The thematic data consists of storytelling, outdoor activities and reading exercises. Collaborative discussions have been the mainstay for analysing and presenting the data and information developed in the study. In fact, outdoor activities and reading exercises helped me to connect the hermeneutic conversations to real life experiences. For example, engaging Brandon in bird watching at the Kortright conservation centre helped me to observe and connect our experiences to what others have written about the influence of bird watching on child learning skills. Revisiting the conservation parks with Brandon helped to clear up the ambiguities and inconsistencies in the data and information collected. Reading the information developed in the study to Brandon allowed him to validate information he agreed with or correct areas of the study he found erroneous.

The thematic analysis explained how data about my experience with Brandon were analysed and developed into text. The data acquisition drew heavily from thematic reflections for analysing the data and developing the information into the study. Thematic analysis is commonly used in humanities, art and literary studies for introducing structure and giving focus to a textual work (Van Manen, 1999). The literary meaning of a "theme" refers to a subject matter or an idea that frequently appears in a text. Themes often characterize ideas and images in music, drama and some scholarships (research?) to capture the essence of a creative work. Thematic analysis in the human sciences helps us to control and structure our lived experiences as we convert our storied lives into text.

The thematic work helped to develop the phenomenological analysis alongside the data collection. This allowed the study to have organization as well as focus. The thematic reflections made it easy for data acquisition and analysis to occur simultaneously and informed the study by helping to develop the main arguments in the study. Several memos and monthly reports were developed from publications on autism, artefacts, photographs, psychological reports, journal entries, and audio and video recordings of important events. The data were reviewed to allow rudimentary coding schemes to develop the study and also to construct knowledge from the data as new findings emerged. The strategy was effective in each of the major coding schemes developed. The coding process supported the thematic focus (nature and music), and at the end the data collected reflected the central idea of the study (Glesne, 1999). I successfully completed the coding scheme by working with a coding log. I earmarked each major code with a number and a page number and also names of the sub-codes as a way for making meaning of their relevance to the study.

The coding scheme started at the beginning of the data gathering process to allow the fieldwork to become a structured manuscript. I analysed the data collected by applying multiple data collection methods through the use of multiple sources and investigators, and from multiple conceptual and theoretical perspectives. For example, I extracted data from personal life stories, oral histories, shared narratives, and journal writing. These multiple ways of knowing helped me to complete the data gathering in conjunction with the thematic analysis. The multifaceted data gathering process helped me to check the authenticity and coherence of the information collected in order to develop the study.

ISSUES OF BIAS

As a researcher, I found it necessary to define my participant role in the study by identifying the ethical boundaries where this study was situated. I understood that phenomenological study is similar to action research where the relationship between the researcher and the researched repeatedly reveals itself. For example, storytelling helped Brandon and me to communicate our experiences and validate or reject the stories we told of ourselves. As Van Manen (1999) suggests, phenomenological study always involves a personal engagement and we are reminded to be aware of what we are engaged in, who we are and what we want to achieve as researchers. Phenomenological research is not without its share of ethical questions and duty implications. I recognized my researcher role as primary, and participant observer duty as secondary. Reading my notes to Brandon for his approval on several occasions dispelled any conflicts that might have arisen from my researcher responsibility and participant observer duties relating to this phenomenological research. The recognition of the ethical boundaries between researcher and participant observer roles helped to develop a self-consciousness that helped me to monitor my behaviour. It also prevented me from any inappropriate practices such as infusing my personal emotions, and holding back any egocentric opinion that might have arisen in the study.

THE RESEARCH QUESTION

This study seeks to make meaning from two phenomenological experiences that have inspired the development of this study. Nature and music are the preoccupying experiences that have influenced Brandon's learning in extraordinary ways that are not yet represented in established concepts. The first phenomenon is Brandon's attraction to nature and nature education. The second experience is the influence of birdsongs and music on Brandon's learning skills. The interplay of these phenomenological experiences has been very much my experience with Brandon's learning behaviour. It is fascinating to see how his preoccupation with nature and music has influenced his socialization and academic work skills. My graduate work has given Brandon and me the opportunity to reflect on these phenomena and to make meaning of them. The dominant question that inspires these phenomenological experiences is: what has been the influence of nature and music on Brandon's learning skills? This study offers the opportunity to uncover meaning from Brandon's experience with nature and music learning. Is it nature and music or is it working from and within a child's deep interest that is the key? For Brandon, music and nature are the keys for unlocking life, learning, laughter, and love!

SUMMARY

The phenomenological hermeneutics was selected for this study to discover in Van Manen's words the "theory of the unique" (Van Manen, 1999). My experience is unique because it is embedded in naturally-occurring phenomena. The methodology and data gathering process were developed alongside Brandon's experience of naturally occurring activities such as watching schools of birds flying freely in the skies. Demonstrating to Brandon how bird sounds could be mimicked appealed to his interest and it encouraged him to engage in critical thinking. The phenomenological study has led a father researcher to discover himself and educational activities that have made a difference in his autistic child's social and cognitive abilities. The multiple sources of information have helped in the synthesisation of the data collected and they have made the phenomenological process sensitive to the concerns of both the father researcher and the researched subject. Another important aspect of conducting a multiple data gathering study was to enhance my ways of knowing and acquiring information.

CHAPTER 4

THE INFLUENCE OF NATURE AND MUSIC ON BRANDON'S EMOTIONAL BEHAVIOUR

A Case Study

If your baby becomes fussy, what will you do? Try some of the following techniques, or perhaps a combination of them, to soothe your baby. As you offer comfort, pay attention to what your baby is trying to tell you. Through trial and error, and with loving patience, you'll soon discover together which soothing methods work best. (Biasella, 2008, p. 1)

Studies suggest that little is known about how children with autism address their emotional problems. Kamio and colleagues (2006), and Jemel and associates (2006) argue that ways to address emotional difficulties demonstrated by autistic children are hard to come by. They observe that children with autism's emotional challenges are influenced by their state of minds.

Lukas and Ross (2005) argue that zoo experiences positively influence a child's behaviour, explaining that zoo interactions can improve a person's emotional behaviour. Not much information is available whether zoo experiences are able to help autistic children deal with their emotional difficulties. In this study, I discuss how zoo learning positively influenced Brandon to improve his emotional difficulties. I offer insights into his zoo interactions and how the experience has helped him to learn about himself, his relationship with others, and his place in the natural world.

The chapter discusses how Brandon first expressed his emotional problems and how we learned about them so as to be able to respond appropriately. During the course of this study, I elaborate on whether his zoo learning experience has contributed in any way to improving his social and cognitive skills. In this study, it has been observed that he only expresses himself through crying and it has been his preferred way of communication with others. The behaviour remained in his preschool years and distracted him from learning new skills. As he grew older, his emotional troubles became more evident and a strategy was urgently needed to respond appropriately to his needs. Jemel, Mottron and Dawson (2006) observe that emotional challenges in autistic persons are one of the less developed areas in education research.

I divide this chapter into three sections to provide a phenomenological description of my experience regarding the influence of birds and birdsongs on Brandon's emotional experience. In the first section of this chapter, I provide a "Father's Story: Brandon's Emotional Experience. It is a narrative account of how I learned for the first time about the role birds and birdsongs (chickadees, bald eagles, and woodpeckers) play in Brandon's behaviour. Through conversations, outdoor activities, and reading exercises, I was also able to identify the connection between birds and birdsongs and Brandon's emotional skills. In the next section of this chapter, I elaborate on "The Zoo Experience," which describes how his fascination with birds led this study to explore his interest in zoo learning. I share my experience of how he gained a sense of self from his visits to the zoo. In the final section of this chapter, "Connecting Zoo Learning to Emotional Literacy" I discuss how the zoo experience provided him with the requisite tools to improve his self-esteem and social skills. For the first time, I learned how zoo experiences positively influenced his emotional behaviour.

A FATHER'S STORY: BRANDON'S EMOTIONAL EXPERIENCE

It is June 27, 1993, Brandon is three months old, and it is about four in the morning. He has woken the entire household with a deafening cry. The sizzling heat had forced me to open up his bedroom windows to allow fresh air into his room. You could hear the birds singing from the trees behind our house through his bedroom windows. Among these shaded trees are the maple trees that have attracted a variety of migratory birds to the neighbourhood. I realized that the sounds of the birds have woken Brandon up and he was lying on his bed crying while he stared at the windows.

I picked him up and held him in my arms with his tummy pushed tightly against my chest. I wanted him to go back to sleep because he had to go to the nursery school at eight. I was worried that if he did not get enough sleep, he would not be able to endure the rigorous school schedule. I decided to employ a few techniques to put him back to sleep. I straightened up his bed and restored his pillow, but he would not sleep. His crying grew louder; it was almost five in the morning. I turned on the light and quickly rushed for his food in the fridge, warmed it up in the microwave and fed him but he kept on crying. I picked him up and undressed him, took him to the bathroom and gave him a warm bath but he would not calm down. I began to think more creatively about how to calm him down.

I held him face down over my forearm with his head on my elbow and my hand wrapped around his thigh walking him across his room. As I passed in front of the open windows to prepare my next course of action, Brandon, hearing the birdsongs from the windows, looked into my eyes and smiled. I stopped for a moment and looked back at his gleaming eyes trying to understand what he was telling me. After five minutes of gawking in silence, he fell deep into his sleep. The experience we gained from interacting with the birds on the trees began to unfold. (Osei, journal entry, 1993).

My first experience with Brandon's emotional difficulty that early morning in June introduced me to his ways of compromising, socializing and learning. At age four, he was diagnosed with GDD and PDD, and it was difficult to communicate with him and understand what his needs and expectations were. His appeal to birds and birdsongs provided me with tools to explore his experience in autism. In fact, his connection to birds and birdsongs provided a clue as to how he communicates and learns. Another important experience to emerge from our interactions that morning was the level of attention he gives to the birds and birdsongs.

Finding myself in the complex world of autism, I began to look for ways to address the emotional and behavioral problems associated with the condition. I began reviewing articles, books, Internet information and newspaper articles, attending workshops and speaking with many parents that have experience with raising a child with autism. Each of the experiences directed my attention to inconclusive, abstract and impractical sources of information (ABA). As I struggled for an answer, I reflected on my experience with Brandon and the birds that early morning in June.

The experience brought many ideas into my mind. In my imagination, I would take him for a walk in the park and engage him in bird play. I would point to a bird, and explain in simple words what the bird was doing at that particular time. Eventually these things happened. I would say to him "bird eats" or "tree grows," and he would repeat after me "bird eats" and "tree grows." I would intentionally replace the words with new words once I was satisfied with his proficiency. At age six, he had mastered the use of several descriptive words. For example, he could describe and explain in several words or in a phrase what activity a bird was engaged in. He would use words like: "bird sings or bird eats." He always enjoyed interacting with birds, but there was one bald eagle in the park that always attracted his attention with their mocking sounds. By identifying his interest in birds and birdsongs, we were able to learn together and understand what we want to achieve.

Brandon's emotional difficulties became a major problem for his nursery school teachers. In his nursery school report, Brandon's teachers observed that "Brandon is beginning to make his basic wants and needs known through short easily understood sentences or phrases and sometimes crying" (Johnson, Dobbin & McNeil, 1997, p. 2). However, there was verifiable evidence to explain what Brandon needed and why he behaved the way he does. Brandon's crying was a way to express his emotional challenges. It was also a way to express his disagreement with things he found unacceptable. His mood changes made his transition from preschool to community schooling difficult and the problem was undermining his classroom performance. His difficulty in controlling his emotional behaviour worsened when he got to grade four. What should we do as parents? It became urgent for us to help him to improve his behaviour if he was to succeed in school. The question we confronted was what was the right course of action to pursue to be able to help a child with autism to learn the social rules necessary for improving his relationship with his peers?

In November 2002, we received his provincial report card and his classroom performance required that as parents, we act urgently to prevent his behaviour from worsening. We learned from his teacher that:

Brandon is finding the transition to the junior classroom a bit of a challenge. His anxiety tends to be high this semester and we see this in the classroom through his inability to control impulsive behaviour and his resistance to joining activities. We are currently working to help Brandon to cope with his anxiety and hope that, with time and the appropriate instructional and intervention strategies, he will feel more comfortable and be able to attend more effectively to his work at school. (Ansley, 2002, p. 2)

Brandon's teachers worked hard to control his anxiety but his difficulty in under-standing the classroom rules made it difficult for his teachers to work with him. Drawing from Brandon's earlier experience with birds and birdsongs, I decided to invite him to the zoo and introduce him to the experience of learning from zoo animals. My objective was to expand Brandon's knowledge of animals beyond birds and birdsongs to other animals in the zoo. I was also interested to learn with him how animals like camels socialize with people. Another important reason for our zoo visit was to provide Brandon the opportunity to learn about chorus frogs to expand his knowledge of animal sounds. I also expected to introduce Brandon to camel rides and to improve his knowledge of animals. We learn from Bexell and colleagues (2007) that "Visitors to zoos often remark that they enjoy seeing animals such as monkeys or otters because they frequently play" (p. 287).

Brandon's visit to the zoo with his class was the second time he had taken a zoo trip. His first zoo visit was in August of 2002. During this visit, he was attentive and actively engaged in animal play. He did not express any resentment towards the zoo animals. I observed that he had a strong bond with the zoo animals because he kept pointing to an elephant in her cage and he would turn back to me by saying, "daddy big one, big one" and I would respond to him "it is the elephant." His emotional expressions were consistent and his engagement convinced me that he liked interacting with animals. Several months after Brandon's initial trip to the zoo, his recollection of his zoo experience lingered on and it motivated me to introduce him to conservation parks, readings about nature, and engaging him in discussions about zoo animals as well as gardens.

In the next section, I elaborate on how Brandon's primary zoo experience led us to develop further experiences in zoo learning. I connect home activities to zoo learning and develop the information as a way of addressing emotional situations in Brandon's life.

THE ZOO EXPERIENCE

It is June 2, 2006 at 11:05 a.m. when the school bus pulled over to the school's driveway on its way to the Toronto Public Zoo. Brandon's school had invited me to accompany the class because there was not enough parental support for the trip. The zoo trip was very much expected and for months it was talked about at home. It was carefully planned and was to bring two special education classes together to visit the zoo. The trip was carefully organized to expose the children to zoo life. For Brandon, visiting the zoo was more than animal play; he was interested to learn about the various animal species in the zoo and how he can relate to them. The zoo experience also provided Brandon with the opportunity to connect his experience with birds in the park and those living in the zoo.

Before his first trip to the zoo, I told him my own experience with zoo life and how exciting it had been for me. I also shared with him my experience with farm animals such as pigs, birds and cows and how sociable animals are when you get to know them. I also shared many nature pictures with him showing a variety of birds, insects, mammals, and reptiles. I introduced him to pictures displaying birds in the tropical rainforest and their nesting places, and how they live side by side with humans in many communities. In addition, we read many books including encyclo-paedias and stories people have written about their personal experiences in the Amazon and rainforest regions.

A week before our second trip to the zoo, I began to prepare Brandon for what we expected to learn. I was amazed to learn for the first time the long list of names of animals Brandon wanted to see. In order to understand him better, I decided to show him pictures of some of the animals in the zoo. One afternoon, I went to the library to search for information on wildlife. I began to read to Brandon from First Nature Encyclopedia, written by Bingham and Morgan (2006). The book introduced us to a variety of flowers, trees, mammals, birds, reptiles, amphibians, and fish. Brandon learned that mammals breathe air and most mammalians live on land with few living in aquatic habitats. I informed him that birds also have a variety of shapes, sizes, and colours of feathered wings and most birds can fly. There are some birds that can not fly such as penguins. I told him that reptiles rely on their environment for food and body heat. Reptiles and amphibians eat other animals and some live on land and in the water. As we were reading he pointed to the picture of fish and I explained to him that fish live in water and some humans eat fish. Brandon gave the reading his undivided attention as I read to him about life in the animal world.

Brandon's Memory Skills

My concern for Brandon was whether he would remember the information that he gained from the zoo. My uneasiness was real because I have learned from studies reporting about children with autism that their memories are weak. Studies suggest that autistic children have spatial memory; as a result, what they learn today may not mean anything to them once the object they are learning about leaves their sight. The poor working memory hypothesis is drawn from the argument that a specific region of the frontal cortex in autistic children's brains is known to be dysfunctional. Although the information has not been validated, studies have advanced the memory deficit function idea by generalizing that autistic children have dysfunctional working memories. For example, Bennetto, Pennington and Rogers (1996) have observed that autistic children have a memory deficit function that prevents them from processing complex information from everyday experiences. However, Minshew and Goldstein's (1993) subsequent studies refute the universal application of the memory deficit concept as being unverifiable.

Drawing from my own experience of Brandon's learning skills and making meaning from the memory deficit concept, I found that Brandon's way of storing, memorizing and processing information was different from a classic case of a child with memory deficit function. Brandon has an impeccable memory for names of people, places and things that matter to him. This means that if he is interested in the animals he interacts with in the zoo, he will have a good memory of his experience and can store up, memorize, process and employ the information in different learning situations. Another important example is Brandon's primary experience with birds and how he has interacted with them in previous learning situations by demonstrating that he likes learning from birds. In a recent educational assessment report, it was found that Brandon has skills for processing information and completing a task once he understands what is required of him (Boyko, 2007).

I have also observed Brandon in different learning situations where he has demonstrated that he has the ability to store information for future use. For example, when Brandon and I explored information on wildlife, birds and marine life, I observed him spreading his arms and hands in the air in a fly-away position, signalling the running around of birds on the outside lawn. He pointed his index finger to his eyes to remind me of the dusky eyes of juvenile mocking birds and how they use their eyes to fly from place to place. Such nature interactions were socially and cognitively productive because they kept us connected as we learned about ourselves and our interdependence with animals.

Based on my experience with Brandon's learning skills, I was confident that his experience in the zoo would help us to understand how he learns and develop a strategy to address his anxiety in the classroom and other learning environments.

The Experience of Animal Naming

Brandon was excited when we visited the rainforest section of the zoo where a variety of frogs were accommodated. He was thrilled to see the different shapes, sizes, colours, and sounds of the frogs and the toads but it was the names of the various animals that triggered his irregular facial expressions. He pointed to a red-eyed tree frog held up between two logs and the frog was trying to leap for safety. At first, I thought the frog's swollen fingertips had made him cringe but I was wrong; he wanted to know the names of the frogs. My experience of Brandon's incredible memory reminded me to be careful with my responses to his questions and not to tell him things I was not sure about because whatever I say, it would stick in his mind.

He was surprised to learn that the frogs he admired were socially labelled in the zoo. Brandon's facial expressions and his silent disposition suggested that he was disappointed with the names given to the animals. At one instance, he pointed to a frog in the pond and I said to him "that is a crazy frog." He responded, "No, no crazy." His eyes looked serious. He moved a step away from me and he yelled at me for the second time, "No, no, crazy." I tried to calm him down but he kept saying, "No, no, crazy." I did not understand why Brandon was protesting against the names of the frogs. I wondered whether he was being stubborn. I recognized that he was looking for the real names of the frogs. At this point, I had no recourse but to find him the proper names of the frogs.

How could the zoo describe animals with epithets such "crazy frogs," "jungle bugs," "stinky ferrets," "wild turkeys," and "weird woods?" I tried to explain to Brandon that the zoo has given the animals nicknames so that zoo visitors could easily identify the animals. I tried to convince Brandon that nature books may provide him with appropriate names for the zoo animals he wants to know about. We explored an encyclopaedic nature book authored by Bingham and Morgan (2006) for the correct names of the zoo animals we had met at the zoo. Brandon was curious to find the appropriate names for the frogs and I was looking forward to finding them for him. To our surprise, the information provided by Bingham and Morgan (2006) was not different from what we had learned from the zoo. The book promoted a comprehensive list of animal epithets, which suggested that animal labeling had been an institutional effort.

These epithets send the wrong message to children about nature. Many nature educators including our public zoos have approached nature and nature education in a teleological manner where organisms are negatively characterized and can give children conflicting views about nature (see Appendixes F and G for examples of the conceptual contestation in nature education). In certain situations animal species have been characterized by their socioeconomic worth. The deliberate introduction of epithets shows how the erroneous naming of animals has negatively influenced children's understanding of nature. Brandon was displeased with the animal naming in the zoo because he knew that frogs are not crazy and turkeys are not wild and he found the epithets problematic. Brandon was disappointed with Bingham and Morgan's account of wildlife and their support for the social labelling of animals.

In June of 2008, we enrolled Brandon in a summer camp organized by Autism Ontario. Brandon and his group visited the Toronto zoo as part of their camp activities. The campers were dismayed by Brandon's impeccable knowledge of frogs and his strong passion for interacting with them. Alyssa (one of the camp coordinators) observed the following activity, "Today, Brandon went to the zoo. He was excited, becoming tired by the end of the day. He particularly enjoyed the frogs and the monkeys. He ate very well. The frogs in particular served as a positive stimulus for him" Alyssa (2008). Alyssa's account indicated to me that Brandon's confrontation of the epithets given to the zoo animals convey the positive approach he takes to nature and nature education.

CONNECTING ZOO LEARNING TO EMOTIONAL LITERACY

At the zoo, we discovered that Brandon enjoys nature learning but his teachers did not understand the level of his curiosity and thoughtfulness about nature. The zoo experience revealed to us that Brandon's deep ecological interest had been taken for granted. In the zoo, he interacted with a variety of animal and plant species and he did not shy away from discussing his ideas about the animals. One year has passed since our last visit to the zoo, and I was surprised to hear him relive and retell his experience with zoo life.

He poignantly described his experience with the elephant he interacted with in the zoo. He remembered that the elephant on one occasion had stretched out her long nose to suck water from a pool. He remembered observing the elephant using her long curling trunk to squirt water onto its back to take a shower. He was stunned to learn about the ingenuity of the elephant and the natural skills the animal possessed. In Dennard and Boles' 1993 study, we learned that elephants could be trained to pull, push and carry loads. Brandon gained a lot of knowledge from his interactions with the elephants in the zoo. For the first time in his life, he thought that if elephants could clean themselves then he must be able to do likewise.

He gained self-confidence to engage in an activity that he was passionate about and that is to learn with animals in the zoo. Realizing his capabilities and his desire to improve on his limitations, I agreed to his request to allow him to bathe by himself the next day after our visit to the zoo. He tried with difficulty but I was amazed by his courage and willingness to do bathe himself, something he had never tried to do before. The zoo visit was already producing educational benefits.

Brandon found the elephants amusing because he would clap his hands and they would respond by stretching their noses. He was amazed to learn that the African elephants are the largest land mammal on the planet, and that an elephant can consume about 300 pounds of food in a day. Autistic students' interactions with nature have not been adequately explored in field studies; ways need to be found to help them develop creative thinking. For example, many children learn about nature from books, films, or participate in classroom discussions, but not through field studies because educators and researchers assumed that such knowledge goes far beyond the imagination of a child. For this reason, many children are not given adequate opportunity to interact with nature and allowed to learn through experience as a means to self-empowerment.

Falk and Dierking (1998) have argued that zoos offer children a meaningful place for learning. Some scholars have even suggested that children's nature learning occurs naturally in nature sites such as the zoo (Kola-Olusanya, 2005). While many studies have affirmed the importance of zoos as learning sites, few studies have investigated the way zoos are presented to children and the impact the information has on children's understanding of the natural world. My experience of Brandon's interaction with zoo animals indicated that the zoo offered him a tranquil place for learning new skills.

Brandon's diagnosis of GDD and PDD changed the way we interacted with him at home. We believed what the professional experts told us about his situation and what we should expect from him. As parents we had hope for his progress and we did not lower our expectation for him. However, people who misunderstood his behavioural differences often would tease him with words like "crazy, weird, and stinky for the things he would do inappropriately. At age five, he was familiar with epithets. As he grew older, he rejected epithets used against him or others. Whenever someone described him as crazy or weird he would say "no, no crazy or no, no weird."

In one of my trips with Brandon to the Toronto Zoo, we came across names such as "wild turkey," "stinky ferrets," and "oven birds" (Osei, Journal entry, 2006). The male turkeys are described as wild because they are big and behave aggressively toward their female counterparts. The male turkeys would puff up their feathers and fan out their tails while walking back and forth in an aggressive mood to find a female mate. The stinky ferrets are described as stinky but friendly towards people, but they do not get along well with female partners. The oven birds make their nests on the ground and the birds make a roof from grass to cover the eggs from predators. Animal labelling does not adequately inform children about what they should know about animate life forms. In my trips to the Zoo with Brandon's class, he pointed to the wild turkey and he expected me to explain to Zhim what that fancy name meant, but I could not adequately explain why some animals are described fancifully and others are not. The exotic names confused Brandon's understanding of animal life.

Muller-Schwartze (1984), Bingham and Morgan (2006), and Yong-Yeon (2000) have mischaracterized penguins in their scholarly works with descriptive words such as "flightless," and "fat and imaginary." These negative epithets are reproduced in children's literature and they confuse children about their understanding of animals. The descriptive ecological character of a penguin in nature literature is beyond the domain of nature learning and does not inform the child about his own connection with the animal life. Nature learning is about human connections to nature and not the opposite. In nature learning social labeling of animals is of no use to the learner because nature learning is about learning through experience. One could argue that to focus on the exotic and informal naming of animals does not contribute any significant information to facilitating the social and cognitive transformation of children in nature because animal naming is a prescriptive way of learning.

My experience of the influence of animal naming on Brandon's learning skills is one of confusion. Fancy names of animals confuse Brandon's ability to learn about nature because of what he learns about animals in the zoo. When he learned that some animals were described as wild and others as stinky he was puzzled. His facial expression and silent disposition revealed to me that the epithets assigned to the animals did not support what he had learned about animals. My experience suggested that a standard way of naming animals to reflect the overall character of that particular animal would help children to learn. The conventional process of naming animals is adequate for a student like Brandon to learn about animals and their behaviours. My disappointment was not only about his emotional response to the epithets assigned to the animals in the zoo but what he learned from his experience.

Today, when parents and educators talk about children interacting with nature, they look for life in the outdoors. For most parents and educators, the zoo is at the top of their list when it comes to a place where children can experience nature by interacting with animals, but our zoos are not what they should be. Zoos should address the needs of the learner because people come to zoos not only to experience nature but to strengthen their emotional connection with nature. My experience with Brandon's zoo interactions revealed that a zoo offers him the opportunity to interact with animal and plant species. I also learned for the first time that Brandon's emotional relationship with birds extends to animals in general. For the first time, I learned about Brandon's desire to learn from the elephants. The experience taught me that Brandon was aware of his relationship with the animals in the zoo. I also learned that the zoo is a place for developing social skills, such as children learning through animals and expanding their knowledge to other areas of their development.

Zoos should not be a repository of information that competes with children's understanding of nature. For example, I learned from this study that Brandon does not like epithets given to animals. My experience in the zoo revealed that the epithets given to frogs in the zoo motivated Brandon to speak out against the exploitation done to animals by given them false names. Brandon's emotion and emotional expression against unconventional naming of animals indicate that epithets given to animals contributed to his confusion in the zoo. It also was revealed in this study that to some children animal naming is more than learning. In this study, animal naming is an emotional issue because it challenges Brandon's way of learning and his experience with animals. In this sense, animal naming undermines zoos as centres of learning and excellence.

In recent times, zoos have become a place where commercialization of animals through fundraising activities has become a popular practice. Fees for animal naming and other services have become a frequent practice in our public zoos. Brandon's confusion about the epithets given to animals revealed to me that animal naming affects how children learn in the zoo. Shipley (2006) observes that animal naming in the zoo provides an opportunity to raise money to support the maintenance of zoo animals. In most modern zoos, one would find that animals are not only living in captivity but exist as commercial objects. For example, people are allowed to ride on animals such as horses and donkeys for money, and in some cases animals are paraded in game shows to entertain visitors for cash. These exotic activities undermine the essence of nature and nature education.

During the development of this study, it was discovered that Brandon was unsure about what he was learning in the zoo. For example, when he learned that the names given to animals in the zoo did not reflect what he has learned about animals, his facial expression revealed his state of confusion. The challenge to parents and educators is to be able to convince children that animals are not crazy but intelligent beings.

The Penguins

In the field study, I discovered that Brandon's zoo experience offered him several educational opportunities. He learned from his interactions with penguins that the birds have feathered wings but they cannot fly. He pondered and wondered why a bird could not fly. His curiosity remained with him and his interest in penguins encouraged me to explore information from a variety of sources (movies, media documentaries, pictures, nature books, and personal stories) to address the many questions he had in his mind. I was also fascinated to learn that penguins are among the few species of birds that never lose touch with their breeding grounds because they keep coming to the same natural landscape year after year (Deguine, 1974).

Brandon brought his confusion about penguins to the zoo. He likes the sounds penguins make and he wanted to learn more. Realizing his interest in penguins, I invited him to the "Famous Players" in June of 2006, to watch with me the academy award-winning documentary film, The March of the Penguins directed by Luc Jacquet. The film featured penguins in their habitat under conditions that were realistically depicted and not through any film trickery. The film displayed how penguins live in their own ecosystem. The animated scenes in the movie were breathtaking because the movie depicted penguins as species with family oriented values who have adopted a culture of stable parenthood. The movie portrayed penguins as monogamous species and to compare their social order with that of humans was interesting because the movie demonstrated the need to treat animals humanely.

The most important contribution the movie made to Brandon's education was that it supported Brandon's advocacy against the epithets given to the frogs.

Brandon enjoyed the movie and it motivated us to explore the opportunities nature featured movies would offer him. I discovered in the study that he learned many creative ideas from the movie. For example, he learned that penguins are beautiful and friendly birds and they do not pose a threat to human life. Brandon developed an interest in nature centered movies. Brandon learned from the film that most penguins live around the Antarctica, the world's coldest and driest continent. He also learned that penguins depend on the sea for food. He knew about penguins because anytime he would see pictures of penguins he would say "Antarctica," meaning penguins are mostly found in Antarctica. One of our most important experiences I discovered during the field study was how Brandon was inspired by the penguins.

Bonding with Zoo Animals

It has been established in nature studies that nature offers children with disabilities and other impairments a therapeutic treatment (Louv, 2006). Yet, in my interactions with Brandon, I discovered that nature offers him more than a connection with the natural world. For Brandon learning through animals allows him to self-evaluate his actions and limitations and encourage him to learn new skills. In light of my interactions with Brandon, how might we understand his social and cognitive abilities? Can we assume that people like Brandon, who have social and cognitive differences, might have the ability to develop a bond with nature and to use that experience to improve their academic skills?

From my field experience, I learned that conceptualizing nature as therapeutic does not allow people like Brandon to emerge from their experience in nature as autonomous beings. For example, Louv (2006) observes that exposing children with disabilities to nature could be a powerful form of therapy. Such assumptions could negatively influence educator attitudes towards children with autism and other impairments before these children have a clear sense of self with which to articulate their interest in the nature learning process. For example, birds and birdsongs have worked consistently in Brandon's learning experience and they have also been shown to have extraordinary influence on his learning behaviour. When he visited the zoo, he expected the opportunity to interact with animals that were least known to him. He showed considerable interest in elephants, frogs, turtles, and camels. When the zoo tour guide asked us if we would like to visit the nature education centre in the zoo, Brandon's expressions indicated that he wanted to learn more about different animal species. Little did I know that he was curious to learn more about the mountain chorus frog (Pseudacris Maculata) that had been one of the animals that he has been fascinated with since Nursery School.

On our way to the auditorium, the different shades of grey and brown frogs in the nearby pond caught Brandon's attention. The lengths of the frogs ranged from 24 to 27 millimetres. Seeing the smallness of the frogs and their beautiful shaded colours, Brandon whispered into my ears "that one, that one." At that moment,

I knew that Brandon had found his voice. The frogs' vocalizations were unique because they were heard from long distances and for long hours; they vocalized quickly and had higher pitched sounds. I knew that Brandon had questions on his mind that he would like to ask the interpreters but his limited use of words made it difficult for him to express himself freely. His facial expression informed me that he wanted to see the mountain chorus frogs. I asked the interpreters if they could bring the frogs to the auditorium for Brandon to see. The interpreters agreed and they brought six mountain chorus frogs to the education centre for Brandon to interact with. Although Brandon had already learned about the mountain chorus frogs from text books and television programs but he has not had the opportunity to see them up close. When he saw the frogs he pointed to the dark stripe running along the tip of the animal's nose through the eye to the groin and he smiled.

At the zoo's education centre, we learned that the mountain chorus frog has a unique chorus of high-pitched, rising trills and their modulation from a sustained chorale sound makes it easy to distinguish them from others. When Brandon learned that the mountain chorus frog's call has a rate of 50 to 70 times a minute and usually breaks for fifteen to twenty seconds, he was ecstatic. He responded by saying "birds, birds, birds," indicating that he recognizes that there were significant differences between the chorales of birds and frogs. His response also revealed that he had emerged from his experience with animals in the zoo as an autonomous subject, with the ability to construct the self.

Studies have identified the important connection between birdsongs and music. Brandon's interest in birds and birdsongs has contributed positively to his interest in music. For example, Webster (1992) argues that there is confusion about creativity as a concept and what it means in the assessment of music teaching and learning. Studies by Costa Giomi (1999), Kiehn (2003), Burnard (2000), Campbell and Scott-Kassner (2002), and Cohen (1980) and Flohr, J. (1985) have identified musical skills as important tools for developing children's learning skills. Custodero and Johnson-Green (2003) have investigated the transmission of musical skills in the context of human interactions and they have concluded that sound groups are the medium through which "musical culture is transmitted and shared." The observation is consistent with how Brandon has developed his learning skills through his interaction with birdsongs and frog sounds.

The zoo learning offered clues as to why Brandon demonstrates an entrenched interest in music. The field experience explains the connection between Brandon's interest in animal sounds and music. Animal sounds provide Brandon with tools for learning music; through music, he learned to dance, sing, read and draw.

When Brandon began kindergarten he could sing the full lyrics of several songs and he demonstrated his musical talent by singing his favourite lyrics from beginning to end. His singing skills, however, could not translate into functional communication to help him relate to others. His teachers focused on expanding his musical proficiency to improve on his functional communication skills by exposing him to musical videos and pop dances. The idea was to help Brandon match the musical lyrics and rhythms with self-initiated actions. He developed dance skills and he could dance to musical rhythms to demonstrate his understanding of sounds and toning lyrics. These musical skills helped him to sing and develop a musical mind, which helped to improve his communicative skills.

In kindergarten, Brandon's teachers and parents compiled his favourite music for his classroom music library as a way of developing activities to facilitate his functional communication skills. After several months of exposing him to constructed chatty words that have been developed from musical lyrics, he showed significant progress in his use of words to communicate his emotions and expressions. His teachers would record his use of single and double words in the classroom. They also followed with keen interest his pronunciation of words they could not make sense of and they will pass them along to his parents for clarification. Brandon's interest in music provided pedagogic and dialogic consonance in his relationship with his teachers, parents and peers. His self-reconstruction motivated his effective communication and socialization competences to allow him to develop a relationship with his teachers, parents and friends. His interest in nature facilitated his love for music because he understood nature and music as having a natural connection.

Brandon's interest in nature endowed him with singing skills to help him relate to others and make sense of the natural world. This is consistent with Neelly's (2001) earlier work indicating that children could develop their own music-learning competences outside of a family's music culture. Brandon's interest in songbirds helped him to develop attentive listening skills as a way of developing his sense of self and developing an interest in what others were doing. His music skills helped him to discover who he is and how to relate to others.

Natural sounds inspired Brandon to develop listening skills to be able to communicate with others. His attentive listening skills helped him to learn music. He was also able to learn different sounds of birds and frogs, and in so doing, he learned about his connection with his natural environment. Studies have identified the dialogic quality that experiences with nature and nature education possess as a way of drawing out students' creativity in nature. Turner and Friedman describe the role of nature and music in education as a universal cultural expression for dialogue in relation to how one understands others and the social complexity of the natural world (Turner and Friedman, 2004). The symbiotic relationship of nature and music also acts as an information resource for the development of students' academic skills. Natural sounds such as birdsongs inspired Brandon's interest in nature and music by helping him to develop early connections with the natural world.

In pre-school, Brandon had developed an obsessive interest in feeding and listening to singing birds. The voices of birds were far more powerful for drawing out Brandon's passion for music and nature than what he had learned from spoken words. In fact, Butzlaff has observed that students listening to music and being sensitive to phonological distinctions can help them to develop language as well as to read and write (Butzlaff, 2000). We also learn from Austern (1998) about the pedagogic quality of animal sounds and the role "nature's sounds" have played in the development of anthropogenic music and education. Brandon's fascination with nature and music take education beyond the prescriptive classroom to an environment of experiential learning.

My observation of Brandon's fascination with songbirds was that he came to the learning encounter with his own expectations. He wanted to communicate with the outer self through nature and nature education. This self-initiated effort was revealing in the sense that I was compelled to reflect on my own experience in nature as a means of understanding his learning differences.

The Fruit Basket

The fruit basket exercise was one of the most educative ways for helping Brandon to address his learning needs at home. Brandon likes fruits but he had difficulty asking for the fruit he likes to eat. In the field studies, it was discovered that he was curious to see the elephants eating bananas and the rabbits eating carrots. The irony was that at age six, Brandon was unable to identify many fruits and he was also incapable of memorizing the names of his favourite fruits such as apples and peaches. He also was not able to tell the differences in fruits. The zoo experience offered us many creative ideas about how to coach Brandon to identify differences between fruits and how to ask for a fruit of his preference.

Brandon found the fruit basket reading program at home creative and interesting. We would bring home different fruits each week and we would fill the basket on the kitchen table with a wide selection of fruits. The idea was to introduce different fruits in the house each week and have everybody learn about individual fruits and their natural history. For example, each family member would be asked to pick up his or her favourite fruit of the day and, after the selection, we would collectively read the natural history of the fruit selected. Brandon would be asked to pick up a fruit of his choice, and the natural history of that fruit was read to him. We also wanted Brandon to learn about the names of fruits that he saw the animals eat at the zoo. The practice continued until we were all conversant with the natural information of our favorite fruits.

We also learned how to eat and enjoy the fruits as they became a part of our family menu. One basket will normally take 25 apple sized fruits to fill up. As the children grew older, Doris and I changed from reading about fruit to the exploration of seedlings. In the summer, we would visit the local library to search for information about the ecological life of a variety of plants. We would take the information to nature stores in the area and purchase selected plants. The most interesting plants we had ever bought were apple and carrot seedlings. The planting and maintenance of fruit plants involves constant reading and research because there are a variety of natural situations that are at times hard to follow. For example, to increase fruit yield it was important to know climate patterns and pest management at every stage of plant development. We would share the information with Brandon by planting with him and engaging in caring for the plants as they developed. We would also visit nature stores with him and observe different flora and plant species. He enjoyed me reading to him about plants and he was always curious about exploring how long it took for carrots and apples to bear fruits.

Our zoo interactions were one of the most important educational activities we had with Brandon. Brandon learned about the fruits the animals eat and he once asked me if he could feed the rabbit and birds. I answered "no." He was sad and he would not eat that evening when we came home. He was allowed to feed the birds in the park and he thought that he could do the same at the zoo. I promised Brandon that I would help him to develop a garden and plant carrots for the rabbit and horses in the zoo. Our experiences from the zoo helped us to think creatively about how to organize activities at home that would help Brandon learn gardening skills. We decided to develop a carrot garden because Brandon felt that rabbits and horses at the zoo would like to eat some carrots. He wanted his own carrot garden such that on his next visit to the zoo he could give carrots to the rabbits and horses. We learned that carrots grow best in raised beds; therefore together we developed beds and planted carrot seedlings.

The carrot gardening encouraged Brandon to develop an interest in hearing me read to him. I informed him that a gardening guide helps the gardener to develop a productive garden. I read Jackson's (2006) study of carrot gardens to him on several occasions and my experience indicated that he enjoyed the information he learned. We learned that planting carrots is educational and fun because carrots take short harvest cycles (from 80–90 days to harvest). We discovered that carrots grow about an inch in diameter and carrots grow green tops to indicate their readiness for harvest. We learned that rabbits like to eat the green carrot tops. We also learned how to treat the soil with manure and remove clods, rocks and weeds from the carrot bed.

Brandon enjoyed watering the soil and he was taught not to put too much water in the soil. He enjoyed the gardening because he was asked to select a seedling he wanted to plant. We also learned how to plant apple seedlings. For example, Grosvenor (2006) informed us that growing apple seedlings need nutrient-rich and properly managed soil to promote high fruit yields.

Reading to Brandon was a joy and one of the most interesting experiences that I have ever had in my fathering practice. Brandon showed deep interest in what I read to him and the fact that he pleaded with me to continue reading to him even when there was nothing more to read inspired me as a parent-educator to aspire to new possibilities.

Collectively we learned by doing and it helped us to gain practical experience in gardening. The gardening also involved listening to music while we prepared the soil and planted the seedlings. The garden songs inspired Brandon to listen and sing along. Introducing music to gardening helped Brandon to listen to and follow instructions. Different songs were played during gardening and the activity motivated Brandon to learn the songs and to participate in the gardening activity. It was discovered in the study that gardening songs helped us to develop a shared interest in gardening and in the process, we were able to develop creative ideas for the purpose of advancing our collaborative work. As Louv has observed, "like similar studies on stress reduction, this study demonstrated that a person does not have to live in the wilderness to reap nature's psychological benefits – including the ability to work better and think more clearly" (2006, p. 102).

Several studies have identified gardening as one of the most important educational activities to emerge out of studies in autism (Woodward & Hogenboom, 2002).

In recent years, researchers have discovered that nature is more than just the aesthetic beauty of the natural world. Nature brings people together by connecting the home with the school, indoor with outdoor and local with global, and in the process prepares humans for the natural world. The traditional focus on nature and nature education has shifted in recent years from leisure to education. Consequently, studies have advocated the use of nature as a therapeutic tool to address the emotional problems in children with disability, but the integration of gardening in nature learning has encouraged many autistic children to learn by doing. Such an activity would help many children with autism to develop relevant behavioral skills to address the emotional problems in their everyday experiences (Woodward & Hogenboom, 2002).

SUMMARY

The zoo has had a big influence on Brandon's learning skills by helping him to address his emotional difficulties through several learning activities. The zoo provided a learning environment for him to engage his curiosity in nature. Chorus sounds from birds and frogs have helped him to affirm his interest in nature and music and support how he learns through birds and other animal species. His attitude towards zoo animals such as elephants, birds and frogs demonstrated how he learns through animals to improve his social and academic skills. Zoo learning inspired him to learn about animals and to develop appropriate behavior attitudes towards others. His fascination with birds helped him to learn to sing, dance and develop language. These skills were critically important in the advancement of his education. He learned how to interact with a variety of animals in the zoo and the experience helped him to expand his interest to other critical areas in his education. For example, he developed an interest in movies because he liked the March of the Penguins. He also learned about the importance of having a carrot garden and caring for the crops. The zoo experience provided us with several educational activities that helped us to address Brandon's emotional challenges.

The zoo experience revealed Brandon's advocacy against epithets given to animals. His actions motivated me to think seriously about my own relationship with animals and whether I have been treating animals humanely. For the first time, I learned about Brandon's emotional connection with animals and his appreciation of the natural world. I also learned for the first time that the interest Brandon developed in birds when he was 3 months old explained his deep ecological sense of self and ways of learning in the zoo at age 12. Brandon's fascination with the elephants in the zoo was revolutionary because he learned that if elephants can bathe themselves then he also could do the same. From his experience with the elephants, he was encouraged to bathe by himself.

The zoo experience reminded me of Cunningham and colleagues (2003) and Custodero, and Johnson-Green (2003) argument that children's social and cognitive skills will improve once they are asked to become active participants in their education. I also observed in this study that interest driven learning is the most appropriate way for helping Brandon to achieve equity in education. These revelations have proven that there is a need for further investigative work relating to interest based learning and how zoo experiences contribute to the educational development of children with autism.

NARRATIVE OF TOILETING TRAINING

For children, nature comes in many forms. A newborn calf; a pet that lives and dies; a worn path through the woods; a fort nested in stinging nettles; a damp, mysterious edge of a vacant lot – whatever shape nature takes, it offers each child an older, larger world separate from parents. Unlike television, nature does not steal time; it amplifies it. Nature offers healing for a child living in a destructive family or neighbourhood. It serves as a blank slate upon which a child draws and reinterprets the culture's fantasies. Nature inspires creativity in a child by demanding visualization and the full use of the senses. Given a chance, a child will bring the confusion of the world to the woods, wash it in the creek, turn it over to see what lives on the unseen side of that confusion. Nature can frighten a child, too, and this fright serves a purpose. In nature, a child finds freedom, fantasy, and privacy: a place distant from the adult world, a separate peace. (Louv, 2006, p. 7)

In the previous chapters of this study, I provide various aspects of my fathering experiences in nature and music. In this chapter, I explore the experience of the influence of birds and birdsongs on Brandon's toileting skills. Drawing from my experience of farm life, I discuss how my father used his interest in animal life to teach me social skills. In turn, I provide a phenomenological description of how my interactions with my father helped me to advance Brandon's obsessive interest in birds and birdsongs. I describe how we developed a common interest in birds and birdsongs to help him develop personal care skills.

Considering the complex nature of autism and its ability to restrict one's ability to communicate, socially interact, and respond appropriately to one's surroundings, it was important to follow Brandon's first interest in birds and birdsongs. His interest in birds and birdsongs has helped him to overcome some barriers that he confronted in school. On this note, I explore how his experiences with birds, birdsongs and music became transformative tools to help him socialize and develop personal care skills. These skills were critically important for advancing his educational goals.

In the previous chapters, drawing from Hawkins (1682), Head (1997), and Turner and Freedman (2004), I advance the conception that nature and music are tools for learning. In this chapter, I discuss my experience of birds, birdsongs and music as tools that helped to educate one autistic child to acquire toileting skills. I also discuss ways in which birds, birdsongs and music helped me as a father to understand how Brandon learns.

This chapter is divided into three main sections for the purpose of reporting my experience of the influence of nature and music on Brandon's learning. In the first section, "Outdoor Activities: How Brandon Connected with Birds and Birdsongs,"

I discuss how Brandon's obsessive interest in birds and birdsongs became tools that were used to develop a common language in his toilet use training. In the next section, entitled "Birds, Birdsongs and Music: Tools for Brandon's Toileting Skills," I report how birds, birdsongs and music motivated Brandon to develop toileting ethics. I elaborate on the difficulties that his lack of toileting skills created for his teachers and for him to access the opportunities in education. In the final section, "Birds and Birdsongs as Tools for Learning," I consolidate the knowledge that birds, birdsongs, and music have pedagogic zeal for inspiring Brandon to learn and improve his classroom skills.

OUTDOOR ACTIVITIES: HOW BRANDON CONNECTED WITH
BIRDS AND BIRDSONGS

On February 12, 2002, Brandon and I first visited the Kortright Conservation Park and we experienced one of the most important educational events that would transform our lives. My reason for bringing Brandon to the park was to give him the opportunity to experience the splendour of birding and gardening, and to learn about a variety of flowers and birds in the park. When we arrived at the park, Brandon's first attraction was to the bald eagles and the woodpeckers that were resting on the trees next to where we stood. He was fascinated with the diverse sizes, shapes and colours of the birds he saw. His excitement was evident in his attentiveness to the sounds from the birds and to the other naturally occurring activities that dominated his environment. He was amazed to see the many ways in which birds used their beaks to prepare food, eat, mimic sounds, and build their nests.

Cages and Feeders as Tools for Learning

In the park, one may wonder why are there cages built for the birds? Birds spend most of their time on their wings in search for food but they also need a place of comfort where they could rest and protect themselves from predators. The apple tree branches cut to fit inside the cages offer the birds' peaceful environment for perching. When I saw the cages in the park I wondered why birds would need cages but after brainstorming for a while and seeing the birds resting their feet comfortably on the variety of perches in their cages the whole exercise made sense to me. I pointed to a bird in one of the cages and I said to Brandon, "this is the bird's home." He did not share his thoughts but I presume that it was the first time he had seen a home made for a bird. Several ongoing activities in the park kept our eyes busy and minds curious.

The bright pink coloured feeders immediately caught Brandon's attention when we entered the bird sanctuary in the park. The gardens where the feeders stood added to the beauty of the park. There were several flowers hanging over the feeders to beautify the landscape where the units stood. The feeders had big glass tubes measuring about eight inch in diameter and they held over a quart each of sunflower seeds. The feeder base had large round trays with raisins that offered resting places for the birds to dine. The variety of plants, insects and birds filled the park with a startling phenomenon that would capture any child's wildest imagination. The diverse colours of the plants and flowers added to the beauty of the park.

Brandon was curious and overwhelmed because he never saw schools of birds dining together. He tapped my hand and pointed to the bald eagles, and he turned his head around and touched his nose and lips to indicate to me that he was experiencing something phenomenal. I could see the happiness in his eyes and his inquisitive mind. I could sense that he had questions in his mind that he wanted to ask me. I realized that the colours, shapes, and lengths of the birds' physical features had appealed to his attention and he was curious to learn more. I learned from his behaviour that he wanted me to explain the naturally occurring events he was experiencing. He pointed to the bald eagle and I responded that the bald eagle is a beautiful bird and birds with similar bodily features often behave alike and share similar habitats. We often identify bird behaviour from their physical appearances. For example, birds' physical features inform us how they live and adapt to their environment. He was not satisfied with my answers and he kept tapping my hands as if he expected clarity from my statements I have made. I realized that he had more questions than I could answer.

At this point, I provided the information that I thought he was looking for. I told him that birds come in a variety of colours and they have different interests, needs, and capabilities. I also told him that they have different shapes, sizes, and physical features that help them to adapt to their environment. I informed him that beaks help birds to eat different foods, protect themselves against predators, and live in different habitats. He smiled but I could see that he was not satisfied with the answers. In fact, for the first time, I was ecstatic to learn about Brandon's attentive listening skills and how he was using this intrinsic tool to learn.

Reflecting on my experience with birds, I began to examine my interactions with Brandon closely. For the first time, I was amazed with his obsessive interest in birds and how he wanted to learn through birds. I began thinking about how my own experience with birds had influenced my learning skills and how the nostalgic feelings continue to echo in my thoughts. This childhood reflection dominated my mind as I mused over creative ways to develop educational activities involving birds with Brandon to improve his learning skills. I realized that if I was able to organize a birding activity that he liked, I would be able to help him acquire the learning skills that he deserved and needed to improve his overall social and academic performance.

Developing Dialogue in the Park

Brandon's interest in birds and birdsongs first came to my attention when he was three months old. My experience convinced me that if his curiosity in birds and birdsongs could be developed and sustained he could possibly learn new skills. My hope began to weaken when he reached six, because he lacked self-help skills and he continued to wear a diaper. We expected that he would be toilet trained by age four because he was able to eat by himself, learn new songs and sing them before his third birthday but he was unable to acquire toileting skills even after several years of coaching. While his skills in areas such as eating, dancing, learning new songs, singing, word usage and his memory for names were developing faster than we expected, he had difficulty in developing personal care skills.

His fascination with birds and birdsongs encouraged me to invite him to the park and introduce him to the natural science of birds. It was the first time we had come to a conservation park not only to learn about birds and their ecosystem (bald eagles, woodpeckers, and chickadees), but also to develop a medium of learning for the purpose of coaching him to improve his overall social and cognitive skills.

I was amazed to learn about Brandon's enthusiasm to engage birds in social and cognitive ways. What I did not know was whether I could transform his interest in birds and gardens to promote his awareness in personal care skills. During our visit to the park, the following conversation between Brandon and I ensued:

Daddy: Brandon, look at the white and brown bald eagle.

Brandon: Yes...head. (Brandon then pointed to his own head to draw my attention to the bird's head.)

Daddy: Yes, the bird has a white head... .

Brandon: White head.

Daddy: ...and a yellow beak.

Brandon: Yes... eats fish.

Daddy: Yes, the bald eagle eats fish... .

Brandon: That fish. (Brandon then pointed to the bird's beak.)

Daddy: ...and poos in her cage.

Brandon: This one. (Brandon then pointed to the birdcage.)

Daddy: The bald eagle eats from the feeder.

Brandon: Yes, there. (Brandon then pointed to the feeder.)

Daddy: Yes, they eat a lot of fish from the feeder.

Brandon: That one. (Again, Brandon pointed to the feeder.)

Daddy: The bald eagle has yellow eyes... .

Brandon: Yellow eyes... .

Daddy: ...and yellow feet... .

Brandon: Yes.

Daddy: ...and flies very fast.

Brandon: Yes, flies fast.

Daddy: Do you like the bald eagle?

Brandon: Yes... yes... (Brandon's pitch of voice changed.)

Daddy: Well done, boy.

It is unfortunate that Brandon's enthusiastic engagement, interest, and expressions in our conversation could not be captured in print because then our story would be consumed by an endless interpretation of non-verbal expressions and responses. My interest was not to assess Brandon's competence in bird ecology, but to extrapolate the educational element in our conversation and to remind him in the future of our experience in the park. My challenge was to take advantage of what Brandon might learn from the bald eagle and organize the information as a training tool to improve his personal care skills as well as to develop other learning skills. My observation was that he found his interaction with bald eagles as a means for understanding who he was and what he wanted to become. From our conversation, there was evidence to suggest his clear communicative and emotional expression. He demonstrated his clear sense of self and he resisted any effort that contradicted his sovereignty of self.

Expanding Brandon's Interest beyond Birds

For the first time, I realized that his understanding of birds went far beyond his interest. He was keen to learn through birds because they offered him a learning space to engage his imagination. It also reinforced his understanding that birds are his tools for learning. I realized that Brandon sometimes behaved unintelligibly but in the above conversation he appeared to be advocating for the kind of learning activities that he deserved to succeed as a learner. For Brandon, birds and birdsongs were a means for engaging his innate abilities to overcome the constraints that society and autism had placed on him. His understanding of the bald eagle indicated that he had experienced an educational event and he was ready to build on that knowledge. Brandon's interaction with birds offered him ways to transform his learning environment. It was obvious that birds offered him a temporal space for improving his learning skills. We also learn from the conversation that he likes birds and he recognizes their role in his educational development. Brandon agreed that the bald eagle was a beautiful bird but he also recognized that bald eagles are predators. The experience informed me that Brandon had a clear sense of self and he was ready to advance his social and academic skills.

My experience in the park provided me the tools to develop a common language with Brandon, even though he could barely speak, play and show interest in what others were doing. The experience transformed my relationship with him because for the first time, I observed that he had initiated the kind of a social activity he was passionate about. I felt proud for resisting the temptation of denying him participation in his educational transformation. Together we resisted the social construction of his difference by allowing him to define who he was and what he wanted to become.

BIRDS, BIRDSONGS AND MUSIC: TOOLS FOR BRANDON'S
TOILETING SKILLS

Since age four, Brandon's difficulties in developing personal care skills had interrupted his schooling. We tried several coaching techniques to help him acquire toileting skills but he found the activities rigid and intrusive, and he mustered his strength to resist them. We discovered that the problem facing us as parents was not limited to finding an appropriate technique to coach him how to cope with his daily activities but to be able to organize an activity that would appeal to his interest as well as ours for the purpose of developing his covert skills.

In his previous school reports, his teachers observed that his limited self-help skills were preventing him from achieving the full benefits of education. As the parents of a six-year old, we realized that without personal care skills he would have difficulty in developing the social skills needed for improving his classroom behaviour. We observed that his limited self-help skills needed urgent attention but how would a child with autism acquire the aptitude for self-care? According to a teacher report, "Brandon's self help skills are limited to feeding himself and depending on his mood, assisting someone dressing him by pushing his foot into his boot, arm into sleeve, leg into pant, etc. We have difficulty getting him to wash his hands and face or allowing us to do it for him (Dobbin et al., 1997).

Brandon's difficulty with helping himself presented serious challenges at home and in school. His frustration at not being able to be self-dependent is expressed in the above report. During the process of developing this study, I observed that if he could be self-supporting his classroom behaviour would improve. The question was where do we start?

As far back as I can remember, Brandon was engaged in activities in the park in a way that I had not seen him behave before. He was talking and asking questions that were interesting and they mattered to him. He was using words that I had never heard him use in conversations. He could now see the bird that he called his friend poo in its cage. It was an exciting moment for a child with autism who learns best when he is put at the centre of the action. It was important for Brandon to learn from his experience, and to expand his knowledge into areas that would help him develop self-confidence. For example, his use of the word "poo" was encouraging for a child who has been having difficulty with his own toilet use skills.

Since our visit to the park, I observed remarkable progress in Brandon's social and intellectual behaviour. He had a clearer understanding of his abilities and limitations, and he was prepared to employ his skills creatively and productively. He would come to me and engage me in a conversation that allowed him to ask questions to address his concerns. Often, he would ask: "Does the bald eagle poo in her cage?" or "Do bald eagles eat in a feeder?" (Osei, Journal entry, 2004).

Here, I knew that his understanding of the word "poo" meant that he was ready to be toilet trained. He followed with keen interest what the birds wanted him to know and his interest in the birds indicated that he was ready to confront his personal challenges. I also knew that if he were toilet trained his self-esteem would improve and help him to make friends. I observed that his memory was good and he could remember a conversation that we had several months ago because he always would say to me "the bald eagle eats from a feeder and poos in a cage." He had a better understanding for distinguishing a feeder from a cage and eating from poohing. I felt that our conversation about the bald eagle would help him to be toilet trained.

Toileting Training: Setting the Stage

On January 1, 2004, Doris and I decided that it was time to put Brandon on a toilet training schedule. We found that Brandon works well with buzzwords and in order for any meaningful toilet training activity to take place we would need to find words that he would remember and use. I knew that words like bald eagle, poo, feeder and cage were important words for bridging the gap between what he can do and what he could not do. I did not expect the change from diaper use to toilet training to be easy but difficult. What I knew then was that with consistency and firmness the task of toilet training him this time would be successful.

With buzzwords bustling in my mind, I had to set the stage for his toilet training to begin. Here, as a father researcher, my interest was not only about cultivating his interest in birds but more importantly, advancing his interest in addressing his lack of toileting skills. According to my literature studies, there was no available information relative to how to toilet train a child with autism; for that reason, we were on our own. Being cognizant of our challenge, we felt that it was necessary to simplify the toileting training process and to deliver the instruction in a way that would make sense to him and make him feel comfortable.

The first step was to go over the conversation we had in the park and to refresh his thoughts on the salient points in our discussions. I reminded him of how the bald eagle had poohed in the cage and liked to eat the raisins and sunflower seeds from the pink feeder. At first, he stared for a moment at me as if he was doubtful but after I had pointed to the birds he looked into my eyes and smiled. Then I asked him, "Is Brandon going to poo in the toilet like the bird poohed in the cage?" My instruction was designed to remind him that his cage was the white toilet bowl and his feeder was his plate on the dining table. I also reminded him that like the bald eagle, Brandon poos in the toilet. He agreed with me, saying that "the bald eagle poos in the cage and Brandon poos in the big, white toilet bowl." (Osei, Journal entry, 2004). From his response, I knew that I was half way through my work. Brandon's love for the bald eagle transformed his learning difficulties by preparing him for toilet training.

The second step was to organize Brandon's washroom in a way that would remind him of his friend, the bald eagle, and the cage. He wanted a picture of the bald eagle on the wall in his washroom. I was able to get him a large picture of a bald eagle without a cage. I convinced him that if he were successful with the toilet training, I would take him back to the park to see the birds and inform the birds how well he has done with his toilet training. My promise to take him back to the park influenced his behaviour in a positive way because he wanted to see the birds again.

Why Pictures did not Work for Brandon

My final plan of action was to organize our conversation in the park into an instructive song and sing it to him anytime he showed a sign to poo. The most difficult challenge was to develop a training schedule that would make the delivery

of instructions easy for him. Every workshop and conference I had attended recommended the use of the picture exchange communication system (PECS). Many parents, educators, and professional providers believed that autistic children cannot learn on their own and they need others to help them learn. What I did not know was whether pictures would work for a child who prefers learning through experience. Brandon was an exceptional child who learns well through experience. PECS uses pictures and print materials to promote communication between children and educators but my experience with Brandon indicated that learning by doing was the best way to make a positive impression on him. In the toilet training exercise, PECS was expected to help Brandon to process instructions by matching words with pictures and print materials. Brandon's teachers and paediatrician advised me to coach him through the use of pictures and print materials because they believe that would make the instructions easy for him to follow. Pictures and print materials were thought to be items that Brandon could use effectively. The Geneva Centre for Autism was very supportive by providing us with pictures and posters that were developed around Brandon's morning routine from the time he woke up to the time he went to school. The PECS captured every activity in his daily schedule. However, according to Brandon's school reports, he was not comfortable with working with visual supports. He preferred to observe activities that were naturally occurring, such as bird watching. He reacted positively to the different birds that he saw in the park. He yelled and echoed their sounds. (Boyko, 2007) I believe that he felt that this activity allowed him to be part of the action.

Using Song as a Coaching Tool

The picture instructions began on November 1, 1996 and continued to December 30, 1999. After three years of using pictorial symbols for toilet training Brandon, he continued to experience difficulty in following basic toilet use instruction. The picture training activity confused him and he showed a sense of nervousness. Following the picture displays, I tried to use direct verbal instruction to help him, but that did not work either. At this time, I decided to develop toilet training instruction into a theme song as a way to help him follow my instructions. Here, I was interested in providing him toilet training instructions based on his experience with the bald eagle. I knew that developing our conversation into a theme song would make it easy for him to understand what he needed to do and employ his skills accordingly. I developed the following tune with words he often hears and uses:

> The bald eagle eats from the feeder laa lala lala lala
> but poos in her cage laa lala lala lala
> white head, yellow beak laa lala lala lala
> yellow feet, brown feathers laa lala lala lala
> Come and sing too Brandon laa lala lala lala
> Brandon goes to the bathroom laa lala lala lala
> and pulls down his diaper laa lala lala lala
> and sits on the toilet bowl laa lala lala lala

Brandon is a good boy laa lala lala lala
Brandon wipes his bum bum laa lala lala lala
with a toilet paper laa lala lala lala
Brandon washes his hands laa lala lala lala
and leaves the toilet room laa lala lala lala
Brandon is a good boy laa lala lala lala
and has done very well laa lala lala lala
Brandon come and sing with me laa lala lala lala
everybody sing laa lala lala lala

Brandon found the lyrics pleasant sounding and he encouraged me to continue to sing even when he knew I had finished. It was interesting to learn that whenever my voice would quiver or the song would end his eyes smoulder. It was an indication that he was enjoying the song and he showed his interest through his facial expression and body movement. At first, I was not sure whether I could sing his favourite song, "The Lady in Red", or compose a song on my own. I played his favourite song to him and instructed him along but the strategy did not work because he knew the words of the songs and he did not want me to exploit the lyrics for toilet training purposes. The most captivating experience from coaching Brandon was how he demonstrated his attentive listening skills to the story of the bald eagle in a self-composed song. Here, the advantage I had was that I could sing to him with lyrics and themes I composed, knew and could control. The richness of the song was that it was organized instructively to achieve a defined task without appearing intrusive and inflexible. Another important experience was that both Brandon and I accepted the song as our common language for achieving our common objective. It was true that the lyrics were organized around Brandon's experience with the bald eagle, and words he knew and would often use, so it was easy for us to work with an instructive song.

The use of instructive songs for teaching students with autism social and personal care skills has not been adequately explored. A careful review of some autism research literature reveals that instructive songs have not been given adequate attention in the education of students with autism. We learn from Brandon's experience that instructive songs organized around a common thematic song could persuade him to learn as well as to assist his teachers to work progressively with him. It was true that our previous efforts were focused exclusively on organized activities and they involved less emphasis on community based alternatives such as exploring a child's interest and developing an instructive song to capture the essential elements of that activity.

Brandon's interest in bald eagles helped him to overcome his uneasiness in developing toileting ethics. The change from diaper use to toilet training was difficult for him but he wanted to succeed because he expected to see the bald eagles again. His fascination with the bald eagles helped him to overcome his uneasiness with the noise toilet flushing makes, or how to decide how many toilet plies he needed to clean himself properly. For example, how does he distinguish the difference between toilet paper and cotton towels? Or the difference between tap-water and water from the toilet bowl? These were challenges that he confronted and which were necessary for him to overcome. To achieve this task, it was important that Brandon understood the differences between objects.

Brandon wanted to use the toilet bowl the same way he saw the bald eagle use her cage. His observation of the bald eagle poohing in her cage reassured him that the toilet bowl was safe as the cage had been harmless to the bald eagle. Brandon demonstrated no strange reaction to the toilet training and he did not go through any repetitive trials that may have indicated his difficulty making the transition. His admiration for the bald eagle's uses of her cage helped him to overcome an important challenge in his development. His teacher recognized his progress in toileting use and she commented that: "Brandon's cooperation during toileting routines has improved this term. He is more careful to pull his pants down completely, lift up the toilet seat and aim in the proper direction. With verbal prompting, he flushes the toilet and pulls his pants up completely" (Thomas, 2002, p. 2).

Brandon's experience with birds had had a positive influence on his toileting skills. His gains in toilet training have helped him to improve his relationship with his peers, which had a profound impact on his academic skills. Thomas (2002) noted that "Brandon has begun to participate more actively during daily music sessions. With coaxing, he is beginning to carry out more of the actions and to occasionally hold up pictograph during a song" (p. 2). Brandon's toileting ethics improved his self-esteem and his willingness to work with others to improve his classroom performance.

Learning through Metaphors

Brandon's experience with the bald eagle and flower gardens stimulated his imagination and offered him the didactic tools for his school readiness. Since his first visit to the Kortright Conservation Park, he would pretend to be talking to the bald eagle on the telephone. He would pick up the telephone and report to the bald eagle that he poohed in the toilet. He took the telephone conversations seriously and he made sure that he reported his achievement that day to his friends, the bald eagles. At times, he would ask me to repeat words and phrases after him and after I responded he would compare my responses to his and select what words or phrases he wanted to use in his telephone conversations with the bald eagles. When Brandon said "white head" I knew he wanted to converse with the bald eagles. My response to "white head" would normally be "yellow beak" or "brown feathers." Sometimes Brandon would say "red head" or "black beak" and I knew that he wanted us to talk about the acorn woodpecker. My responses meant a lot to him because he found that I understood what he was looking for. He found that my answers validated what he said. Gradually, he was able to learn about the ecology of different bird species.

Bird play helped us to organize our vocabulary to communicate with each other as a means for helping Brandon to develop functional communicative skills. I would point to a bald eagle's beak and say "bird's mouth" and I would point back to his mouth and I would repeat "Brandon's mouth" to him several times. The nature training activities expanded over time into areas such as colour identification of bird feathers and bird eating behaviours. The activities helped Brandon to recognize the diversity among birds and it increasingly encouraged him to explore other educational opportunities. He enjoyed feeding and watching birds eat.

A fruit garden offered Brandon the opportunity to learn names of fruits and put the words together into sentences. I would usually take Brandon to a fruit garden that had various berries. I would deliberately select a strawberry or a blueberry and I would say to Brandon, "this is a strawberry" or "that is a blueberry." In some instances, I would do the same thing with a tree or a bird by saying "this is a tree" or "that is a bird." I would work on one item at a time and make sure that he would learn visually and that he would memorize the names of the fruit and the birds. I would quiz him in the same way my father had done with me several years ago, when I was Brandon's age. I would ask him to tell me the name of what I would point to and when he failed to answer what I had taught him to say earlier, the exercises would be repeated until he could develop a mental picture to describe the word to explain what he was looking at. After several repeated exercises, we engaged in a drawing activity to confirm his understanding of the nature exercise. My intention was to teach Brandon about knowing what responsibilities and consequences were involved in growing up in nature.

One of the most important aspects of taking Brandon on nature walks was to improve his ability to identify and learn about the differences in natural objects such as flowers. When we visited the Kortright Conservation Park, I took Brandon to flower gardens and I would ask him to get me white lilies or red roses. Sometimes I would ask him to point to his eyes, nose, and head. Brandon's identification of the bald eagle informed me that he was ready to identify his own body parts. After our nature walks, I would write the names of some of the organisms that we saw. The common names I would write were chickadee, woodpecker, bald eagle, strawberry, blueberry, and apple. These I wrote on a blackboard to assess his understanding of the nature exercise. Usually he would pass the evaluation after he had read to me the names I had written down. The exercises continued until he was proficient and comfortable with the identification and word use drills. The nature drill generated many important benefits. Thomas (2002) observed that "There has been a significant improvement in Brandon's literacy skills this term. Not only is he very much in tune to initial sounds and rhyming words, but he is beginning to develop a sight word vocabulary" (p. 1).

Brandon developed words from his interaction with birds and the experience helped him to expand his interest to classical and pop music. His love for nature's sounds drew his attention closer to music and dance. In music, he developed an interest in dancing and he would competently imitate the "moonwalk" in front of his teachers and peers. Brandon explored nature to improve his understanding of himself and, in the process, opened up his social and cognitive world to people around him. His fascination with the mellowness of natural sounds of songbirds, the varied melodic modulations and gradations from birdsongs and the great brilliancy of the birds' executions empowered him to socialize with birds to make meaning from his experience. His adoration for natural sounds motivated him to explore nature's complexity to address his curiosity and understand his place in the natural world.

BIRDS AND BIRDSONGS AS TOOLS FOR LEARNING

Considering the social and cognitive deficits associated with autism, caring for a child with autism required experience and creative ideas. It also demanded that what I knew was possible came from my own experience. Brandon's interest in birds, birdsongs, and music helped him to develop positively in many areas in his educational development. They also provided a learning space for him to acquire personal care skills to improve his classroom behaviour that had often been an impediment in developing an interactive communication with his teachers. Brandon's teachers expressed the difficulty of communicating with him because he lacked spontaneous communication and his expressions were difficult to understand. Brandon's fourth grade teacher reported that:

> While Brandon is having difficulties remaining focused on most classroom activities, he is now able to stay in and attend to our morning and afternoon communicating groups. His ability to use meaningful spontaneous communication is very limited, while rates of preservative self-talk are currently very high. Brandon requires visual augmentation and calculated lapses of time in order to process the meanings of many words. (Ansley, 2002, p. 3)

There was no doubt that Brandon experienced difficulties in school but from the report we also learn that there was room for progress. The challenge was how to help Brandon to communicate clearly. According to Brandon's teacher, it was difficult to engage him in a meaningful reciprocal communication; that made it difficult for his teachers and peers to engage him productively. According to Ansley, Brandon engaged in "self-talk", meaning that he enjoyed talking to himself. The report offers three important areas of information that made it difficult for teachers and behavioral experts to communicate with Brandon. First, Ansley observed that it was difficult to communicate with Brandon because of his lack of focus on classroom activities. Second, we learn from the report that Brandon attends communication sessions but he engages in frequent self-talk. Finally, Ansley observed that Brandon needs additional time to process information and that visual communication would be helpful for him to develop effective communication skills.

The report identified teacher frustration with Brandon's repetitive self-talk but experience suggested that his communicative utterances, with patience, could be interpreted intelligently to address his needs (Osei, Journal entry, 2005). Brandon's willingness and ability to attend communication sessions was an indication that he was ready to engage his class in a meaningful communication. Here, the teacher's acknowledgment of Brandon's developmental oddities focused solely on what the teacher needed to see in order to understand his actions. The problem observed was that with a disorder as cumbersome as autism, it was important to learn from the student's actions to be able to understand his needs. We learn from the report that Brandon's interests were not actively solicited in spite of his willingness to participate in classroom activities.

We learn from Ansley's report that visual augmentation was a solution for regularizing Brandon's unintelligible communicative utterances, denying Brandon the opportunity to interpret his verbal expressions so that his utterances could be understood. It was an opportunity for the teacher to reach out to Brandon by identifying his interests. The report shows the common mistakes that have been made by experts and many educators who have worked with Brandon in the past. Experts try to impose their preconceived ideas on Brandon, rather than learning from him and identifying his learning style. Studies have discussed the difficulties educators confront when dealing with students with learning differences and they attribute the problem to educators' lack of understanding of the student.

Brandon's interest in birds, birdsongs, and music was identified from my interactions with him. The ability to appropriately engage him came from the experience in my narrative stories that informed me that when a child demonstrates an interest in nature based learning that child can be directed to many creative ideas in nature and nature education. It was observed that teacher organized classroom activities that were outside of the natural world were of less interest to Brandon (Yanchyshyn, 1998). For example, Brandon did not show much interest in learning with toys or pictures of objects, but in activities that were nature- based and naturally occurring he was interested.

At age 12, Brandon had developed an interest in nature –based activities he could count on in times of need. His learning loyalties were the activities that led him to develop additional experience. For example, one strand of learning loyalty was his mastery of bird names and how the experiences helped him to develop the ability to learn names of people and places. He was able to improve his academic skills by engaging birds and birdsongs in ways he understood. At school, he found that birds, birdsongs and music were a way for him to achieve a sense of security and a feeling of inclusion. He discovered that learning through birds, birdsongs and music helped him to expand his perception of himself, others and the world. He prepared for school by drawing from his experience with birds, birdsongs and music and he used the experience as a key for accessing the school curriculum. Brandon's expansive memory of names of birds and words to describe bird activities remained when he started high school.

Another strand of interest was how Brandon learned to listen to bird stories, read, draw, count, dance and sing by drawing experiences from his interactions with birds. He often asked me to describe the colour of a bird's body parts so that he could identify differences between colours. He knew that the bald eagle had a white head and a yellow beak. The exercises continued until he was proficient in identifying colours in his favourite birds. This was important in advancing his classroom work. Over time, he developed expertise in identifying differences in birds and his confidence would motivate him to quiz me on the colouring of birds' physical features.

Brandon was able to improve his academic skills by engaging birds and birdsongs as learning tools. At school, Brandon found birds, birdsongs, and music as tools for learning and making connections. He discovered that learning from birds and birdsongs helped him to expand his social and intellectual skills to understand who he is and what he wants to become. He prepared for school by drawing from his experience with birds and birdsongs and he used the experience as keys for accessing the school curriculum. Brandon's expansive memory of names of birds and words to describe bird activities remained when he started school. According to Brandon's first grade teacher, he already knew phrases such as "bird has a beak" and "birds sing" when they first met. Brandon's teacher reported that his interest in birds and birdsongs were exploited as tools for teaching him social skills and also to get him to attend to his tasks (Osei, Journal entry, 1998). According to his preschool report, Brandon would point to the window whenever he wanted to have his lunch. His preschool teachers were not clear as to why he did this but over time I discovered that whenever he heard something creative in class that he had already learned from his experience with birds and birdsongs he would point to the window. He also made reference to windows whenever he wanted to go out and interact with birds.

At age 12, he was familiar with the ecology of bald eagles and woodpeckers and he could identify differences in their physical features as well as the way they yelp and squeal. As he quizzed me, Brandon would often point to his favourite bird of the day and ask: "What bird is this?" After providing the name of the bird, he would then follow up with a probing question such as: "How do you spell bald eagle?" He would wait patiently for a response and if he was not satisfied with the answer, he would ask the question again. After a series of probing questions, he would end the quizzing by saying: "I like bald eagles," or "I love the woodpecker." My most important observation with Brandon's nature quizzes was that he acquired comprehensive word vocabulary that helped him to develop sentences with words he preferred to use. It also helped him to communicate with his friends and eventually he developed social relations with his peers.

In school, one area in Brandon's schooling where the influence of birds on his learning skills was significant was in visual augmentation. Brandon is an experimental learner. One might have expected that visual schedules would work for Brandon because he has autism but introducing visual augmentation without Brandon experiencing the object of cognition was a difficult task for him. Brandon experienced difficulties in differentiating between colors. Several visual augmentation strategies were used but without success. We found that Brandon's experience at home was preventing him from progressing at school. For example, Brandon was born in Canada but my wife and I are both from Ghana. He enjoys our cultural dishes more than Canadian foods. His favourite cultural dish is rice and spinach gravy and for soup based meals, he prefers fufu, which is pounded plantain eaten with peanut butter soup. When Brandon became 10, my wife and I were interested in teaching him the names of his favourite meals and to recognize the differences between them.

Drawing from ABA strategies, we tried to employ different educational activities, including mental and visual coaching. This strategy did not work. We decided to take one step at a time. For this reason, we decided to bring his attention to the fact that his favourite dish consisted of two main ingredients that we thought were important for him to know and those were rice and gravy. Since there were several types of rice and gravy in our local menu, it was important to help him to differentiate rice and spinach gravy from the other gravy dishes and to be able to clearly express himself. We decided to use pictures to teach him, but as an experiential learner, he preferred to identify the dishes by their colours and to experience what they were. He was able to recognize that rice is white and spinach is green from learning to serve himself at the table. As a result, white and green became his favourite colours.

The white and green colour images reminded Brandon of his favourite dish. In the classroom, he never forgot his favourite colours and when his teacher drew a tree with green leaves on a piece of white paper, the image communicated different messages about what his teacher wanted him to know. For Brandon, the colours reminded him of his favourite food but his teacher wanted him to learn about the relationship between trees and leaves. The teacher's task was to explore ways of communicating the classroom message to him. While his teacher wanted to discuss plant metamorphosis, Brandon thought the message was about his favourite food. Such miscommunications are common when communicating with students with autism; an informed educator can make a difference in bringing greater balance between autistic behaviours and classroom tasks.

Our solution to this dilemma was to go back to the birds. The bald eagle and the woodpecker were Brandon's initial colour training project. They displayed colours that Brandon and I admired very much. Our interactions with the birds helped us to learn about the colours of the birds and the differences between them. Brandon's interaction with flower gardening helped him as well. These tools for learning were important in Brandon's education. While scholars in studies for autism and special education teachers were entangled in conceptual and practice- defining debates about what constitutes appropriate education and instruction for students with autism, the real challenge facing many special education teachers had been how to appeal to the interest of students with autism to develop academic skills.

Reliance on professional services for classroom support has made it difficult for teachers to develop fluid communication with students like Brandon. The solution to this educational impasse is to empower teachers with information that would help them to become researchers in their classrooms without others telling them what to do. Studies have recognized the emotional stress that teachers experience in their effort to communicate with students with autism.

There was no doubt that birds, birdsongs, and music played a significant role in advancing Brandon's classroom skills. Brandon's fascination for the outdoors has been a tool for helping him to learn. In his eighth grade educational assessment, Boyko observed the following behaviour:

When the examiner entered the community classroom on the morning of December 4, 2006, classroom staff reported that Brandon had begun suddenly hitting the teacher in the last two weeks. Brandon was observed to be in the calming room; his visual schedule was on the table. Staff attempted to have Brandon re-enter the larger classroom from the calming room. When asked if he was ready to work with the examiner, Brandon said that he was not ready. When given a choice of an alternate activity, he indicated that he needed to go for a walk before doing his work. (Boyko, 2007, p. 6)

Since then, the school has worked hard to explore the social aspects of Brandon's classroom behaviour. What was missing in Brandon's independent educational program (IEP) was a classroom plan for advancing his interest in birds, birdsongs, and music to help integrate his outdoor interest with classroom learning. In grade nine, Brandon had developed the requisite language to tell his teachers what time he wanted to go for a nature walk to see the birds and listen to birdsongs.

From the report we learn that Brandon's behaviour improved whenever he was allowed to go for a walk. The outdoor activity was more important to him than the classroom behaviour. His teachers observed that whenever Brandon behaved improperly, the only way to convince him to cooperate was to allow him to go for a walk. Louv (2006) informs us that children with social and cognitive impairments including those with ADHD could improve their behaviour with nature activities because nature engages children's curiosity and expands their imagination. Autism is a disorder that remains a mystery. Hence, it is prudent to observe autism children's interests and help develop that information into a national education strategy to inform parents, educators, and service providers.

SUMMARY

Studies have observed that nature can be productive therapy for children with developmental impairments (Louv, 2006). However, there have not been adequate studies done about how nature influences autistic students' readiness for school. What we know is that birds and birdsongs contributed to Brandon's social and intellectual development and helped prepared him for formal school. However, there is inadequate information about how nature and music generally influence autistic students' academic skills. Studies have unsuccessfully tried to identify ways to appeal to autistic children's interests for the purpose of helping them to advance their academic skills. There is an urgent need for helping children with autism improve their learning skills because of the growing challenges in the education of students with autism. This study provides a narrative account of how birds and birdsongs positively influence Brandon's educational development. Evidence suggests that personal stories could contribute significant information to help children with autism succeed in school. These personal narratives of experiences could contribute significant information to the development of a national autism education strategy to inform educators, parents and professional service providers about creative and productive ways for helping children with autism to thrive at home and in school.

CHAPTER 6

APPLICATION OF THEORETICAL AND EXPERIENTIAL LEARNING

It was June 29, 1993, the first full day of summer, and we had just finished three hours of house cleaning. Brandon and his sisters were busy watching Sesame Street, a television program designed for young children. The full-bodied Muppet, Big Bird, performed by Carroll Spinney (1969) was televised on the Public Broadcasting System (PBS) that afternoon. The six year-old bird's journey to Ernie was a game where Big Bird and Ernie had to search for each other in hidden boxes. Brandon's babbles and concomitant excitement communicated his feelings when Big Bird was about to find Ernie. He became silent when Ernie was about to find Big Bird. The self-expressions revealed his happy disposition, thrill seeking, shyness, fretfulness, and impulsivity. The Sesame Street segment was the most successful televised show I found to make known dialogic qualities in a nonverbal child. (Osei, Journal entry, 1993)

From this observation, it would have been impossible not to ask why Brandon was fascinated with Big Bird, and not Ernie. The answer is simple: Brandon's interest in birds motivated him to show sympathy for Big Bird, even though he knew that Big Bird and Ernie wanted each other to hide so they could seek. These Sesame Street stories help us to understand how a nonverbal child learns through facial expressions without using words. Brandon's reactions to the televised stories revealed to us how he responds to educational situations. I observed him with excitement as he led us into the early stages of his communication development. His self-expressions always revealed to us what was going through his mind. For the first time, I learned how he uses signs and nonverbal utterances to communicate his needs. At times, he would express his frustration with vocalization, his curiosity with silence, and his happy dispositions with laughter. I realized that I was experiencing how a child communicates nonverbally and my challenge was to make meaning of those expressions in order to communicate with him. I realized that impulsive actions and creative responses were a medium of communication that he knew and wanted us to acknowledge because he was communicating to us without words. We learn from Freire that "the important thing is to detect the starting point at which the people visualize the given and to verify whether or not during the process of investigation any transformation has occurred in their way of perceiving reality" (Freire, 2003, p. 107). In this chapter, I describe how impulsive expressions and creative responses have been the key to understanding Brandon's learning needs. Brandon's impulsive language and our subsequent parental responses have been the prime communication tools for addressing his social and intellectual challenges.

In this chapter, as a father researcher, I discuss the experience of caring for, communicating with, and coaching a child with autism to help him acquire social and cognitive skills. This I did through my personal observation of his self-expression and non-verbal utterances.

The chapter consists of four sections. First, I provide "A Reflection on Brandon's Impulsive and Receptive Ways of Learning" to explain these ways of learning. Second, I discuss the Sesame Street program to inform readers on how Brandon invited me to experience his style of learning with him. Third, I elaborate on "The Constraints of Autism: A Classroom Experience." Here, I discuss the challenges we confronted in Brandon's classroom, and how we overcame the difficulties in his educational development. Finally, I explain "a teacher's rush to judgment" as a way of sharing my experience of Brandon's learning. I discuss how Brandon taught me to teach him to navigate the complexity of autism and to help him develop his interest in education.

A REFLECTION ON BRANDON'S IMPULSIVE AND RECEPTIVE WAYS OF LEARNING

Brandon's impulsive and receptive languages of learning have not received the attention they deserve in the literature of special education or in the classroom. Autism-related behaviours have presented significant challenges to students' class-room development. A careful observation of Brandon's learning behaviour suggests that he learns through his spontaneous expressions; the responses he receives from those expressions validate his behaviour. As a result, he is encouraged to learn new skills. Unfortunately, the Ontario special education guidelines have not focused adequately on how educators should address the impulsive and receptive ways of learning that autistic students often have.

According to the Oxford Reference Dictionary, impulse is defined as "a sudden urge to act, without thought for the results" (Soanes, 2001, p. 418). Receptive language (see Glossary) on the other hand is the ability to understand information. To pedagogically explore impulses in autism, it is important to capture its definitive interpretation concisely, and that means understanding impulse as a medium of communication that expresses one's experiential desire for a constructive dialogue. In life, impulse allows a person to express his or her authentic self when engaged with others. In essence, I am arguing that through Brandon's impulses I was able to understand his eye contact and other bodily expressions. For the innovative educator, impulses in nonverbal language require the organization of creative pedagogy.

Impulsive expressions in Brandon's early childhood development offered us the opportunity to explore a way to advance his language and academic skills. It also allowed us to help him in his development of who he is and what he wants to become. For example, impulses observed in Brandon's interactions with birds and birdsongs helped us to recognize his interest in nature and music. There was the maple tree in the park behind our apartment building where Brandon and I would take short rests after a long day's work. At the time Brandon was two years old and it was difficult to communicate with him in a way that made sense to him. Brandon's impulsive expressions were initially observed when he saw birds nearby; his expressions brought to our attention how birds and birdsongs appealed to his interests, made him curious and got his attention. The supporting evidence for all this was more pronounced when the birds flew from his view. The babbles and whimpers would begin and communicating with him was necessary for calming him down, but how would one who does not know him do it?

These communicative impulses and requisite responses encouraged his parent-educators to organize creative activities aimed at advancing his social and academic skills. Recognizing his interest in nature and music, we knew how to communicate with him and what to point out to him and where to take him if he was fussing. These domains of thought are what have not been adequately addressed in studies on special education. Understanding nonverbal expressions when educating students with autism and other developmental impairments would help us to understand the needs of students and find the right words for engaging them in communication. Brandon's nonverbal expressions provided me with the opportunity to engage him in educational activities that ultimately helped me to understand him. Reiff (2004) observes that "gaining self-awareness and self-understanding helps students with learning disability increase recognition of their own strengths" (p. 187). These insights are what empower students with learning impairments, and other margin-alized groups, to have confidence in themselves to pursue their educational transformation.

THE SESAME STREET STORY

The Sesame Street educational program teaches pre-schoolers basic life skills such as how to cross the street, personal hygiene, and play skills. The program has had a profound impact on Brandon's learning behaviour. We first understood the meaning of his impulsive and receptive expressions when he watched a June 1993 program. As a nonverbal child, his expressions led us to his ways of learning. Over time, his impulsive and receptive expressions became clearer and we were able to understand how he uses words. Brandon learned how to develop his vocabulary and word usage from the Sesame Street program.

One day in June of 1993, Brandon was watching one of the Sesame Street segments when we heard him laugh excitedly. I drew near and sat down next to him to find out what he was laughing about. I took my journal and recorded his behaviour because it was the first time I had heard him say "ee, ee, ee" and "ha, ha, ha." The nonverbal utterances drew my attention to him because I felt that he was experiencing something unique. I found that Ernie and Big Bird were playing "hide and seek", which was a game where Big Bird was about to find Ernie hiding in a wooden box. When Big Bird found where Ernie was hiding, Brandon broke down into loud laughter (Osei, Journal Entry, 1994). The experience we gained from his interaction with the televised program was important because it helped us to appropriately coach him in activities that mattered to him. These activities helped improve his vocabulary as well as his ability to use the new words. Brandon has watched every segment of Sesame Street since he first saw it. At first, it was difficult to find out whether he understood the story but over time he was able to express himself clearly. His nonverbal expressions were consistent and we discovered that he communicated his needs through gestures, whimpers, laughter, and other social cues.

At times, Brandon used pitch changes in his voice to convey different meanings in his nonverbal expressions. The tone change in his nonverbal articulation indicated which language he was communicating in. A high tone indicated that he was speaking his native language and a low tone suggested that he was speaking English. For example, we found that Brandon used a lower pitch when he said "ee, ee, ee" during his watching of the Sesame Street segment. His tone changed when he was watching a similar Ghanaian movie documented in Twi. Brandon responded in a higher pitch eeeee, eeeee, eeeee. The different tones indicated that his dual language development was important in his educational progress.

Connections to Basic Life Skills

Brandon's nonverbal expressions were a constant reminder of how to engage him in activities that were important to him. His expressions were his advocacy tools as well as his invitation to others to experience his social and cognitive worlds. Because of his limited uses of language and repetitive behaviours, it was difficult for his parents and educators to understand his needs and provide what he deserved and needed to succeed in school. His laughter and whimpers were keys to understanding what he needed and how to address those needs. My experience from the Sesame Street stories convinced me of this.

Brandon's appreciation for Big Bird not only communicated his fascination with birds but showed that he was experiencing an educational event. His uses of gestures, whimpers, and laughter were important educational information that introduced us to activities that he cared about. When he murmured softly, he was expressing his disappointment for Big Bird failing to find Ernie. When he laughed loudly, it was an indication of his excitement that Big Bird was able to find Ernie. Brandon's expressions informed us of how his learning activities should be organized.

His pitch of voice indicated which language he was speaking. Brandon's high-pitched voice informed me that he was responding in his native language and his low-pitched voice suggested that he was responding in English. I have observed tone changes in Brandon's voice when he is under stress or excited about his experience but these grunt changes are usually accompanied by actual mood changes that indicated he was under stress. The impulsive and receptive expressions taught me how to engage him in his attempts to acquire the basic social skills needed for him to successfully integrate into the school culture. I found in Mead (1967), Foucault (1972), and Ricocur (1991) that our sense of self is communicated through language and our experience explains who we are.

When Brandon was three, I observed that his gestures, whimpers, and babbles transformed into words but his silences and happy dispositions continued to play a significant role in his language development. In the Sesame Street program, he found what he needed to succeed as a learner. After his supper he would point to the video recorder indicating that he wanted to watch the Sesame Street. His interaction with the Sesame Street characters over the years brought our attention to the importance of critically examining his expressions so that we could perhaps use them as an information tool for developing creative activities to improve his social and cognitive needs. In Brandon's nursery school report, his teacher observed the following development:

> Brandon is beginning to make his basic wants and needs known through short easily understood sentences or phrases and sometimes crying. The use of the word 'I' is occurring more frequently. Examples of this are: More milk, I want Soya sauce (meaning I want lunch), I want window (meaning want my diaper changed), and I want apples. Brandon does a lot of talking to himself which is not as easy to understand. Speech is more unclear and often repetitive. Tone of voice often changes to match what he is saying and his body language. (Johnson & McNeil, 1997, p. 2)

Brandon's nursery school report indicated that he had made significant progress in nonverbal communication through his use of words and sentences. We also learn that his impulsive and receptive behaviours remained. His teachers observed tone changes in his language, which were often associated with what he was communicating. The teachers also observed that Brandon's self-repetitive talk made it difficult for the teachers to make meaning of what he was saying. Brandon's bilingual languages and language switches often made it difficult for him to be understood. His limited use of words made it even harder for his teachers to work with him.

At home, we knew that Brandon used the pronoun "I" for self-advocacy. For example, he says "I want Soya sauce" to request a break. He would also say, "I want window." In the classroom, his teachers interpreted his words as "his request for a diaper change" but at home, it meant that he wanted to play outdoors. The difficulty for educators and service providers who were working with him to accurately interpret his use of words encouraged us to examine his expressions thoughtfully and make sense of them. Brandon communicated his needs through the word 'I' (Osei, Journal entry, 1997). Making meaning of his nonverbal expressions provided an avenue through which he could be reached even when his expressions were unclear to us.

THE CONSTRAINTS OF AUTISM: A CLASSROOM EXPERIENCE

On February 20, 1997, Brandon was one month away from his fourth birthday when he was formally diagnosed with autism. We observed then that he was less interested in what others were doing. He had withdrawn from many of the activities he had shown interest in before. He had already lost his spontaneous communication skills. His fascination with the Sesame Street episodes seemed to have come to an unexpected end. Brandon would sit in front of the television and watch the Sesame Street show he enjoyed but his impulsive and receptive expressions had disappeared. I knew that if I failed to help Brandon grow successfully, I would have failed as a father. I was confused but the lessons from my father kept saying "not to give up hope." I also realized that my father had never experienced autism the way I had, but my thought of what he might have done in this case taught me patience to learn from a disorder that is shrouded in mystery.

Brandon's lack of reciprocal responses became his teacher's concern. His lack of self-expression had labelled him as "a learner disabled" one that needed remediation, a state of being unimaginable a few months ago (Osei, Journal entry, 2000). I was confused because I did not know what to do. I confronted significant challenges that needed urgent attention. For example, how do I help Brandon integrate into the school community and make him feel a sense of belonging? Brandon's school reports describe some of the difficult challenges that those who worked with him confronted. His teachers observed the following development:

Every couple of days Brandon is doing something new. It may be changes to the way he is talking to himself or to the way he is interacting with others. We feel Brandon is very bright and has a lot of potential and need help in interpreting his actions and developing a program that will help him grow. (Johnson & McNeil, 1997, p. 4)

The single most important challenge to Brandon's teachers was how to interpret his impulsive, expressive, and receptive languages. I recognized teacher frustration in the report but a carefully planned strategy to address the confusion surrounding Brandon's actions was lacking. I observed that Brandon's actions at home were not different from what he communicated in school. At home, however, we had the opportunity to learn with him when he was engaged in activities that appealed to his interests. We knew what he needed when he made certain utterances because we understood many of his expressions. We learned those expressions with him when he was an infant and we understood his needs. The teachers' inadequate preparation made it difficult for them to help Brandon improve his classroom performance. The teachers would have been able to understand Brandon's classroom behaviour if there had been adequate information available to explain his actions. Information about his previous experiences with Sesame Street would have helped those working with him to make progress. In the next section, I describe how my understanding of Brandon's actions helped me to teach him social skills.

A TEACHER'S RUSH TO JUDGMENT

On October 14, 2005, the secretary of Lorna Jackson Public School asked me to come and meet Brandon's teacher and principal. When the call came, I was getting ready to leave home for a noon appointment with a staff member at the bank. The secretary reported to me that Brandon had hit one of his teachers on her wrist and the behaviour was inconsistent with the school's policy. I was asked to come to the school to pick him up and have him spend the rest of the day at home. For me, it meant changing my plans for the day to accommodate the school's request. The first item on my schedule was to cancel my bank appointment. Then, it was time to drive to Brandon's school. I arrived at 11:45 a.m.

When I got to the school, there was an instruction posted on the main school entrance asking all visitors to report to the office. Brandon's classroom was close to the southeast entrance, which is where I had entered. The office was easy to find. It was located on the left side of the main entrance, where I had entered. I entered the office and introduced myself as Brandon's father. The secretary, upon recognizing me, informed me that Brandon and his teacher had left the office and they were in their classroom.

It was exactly 2 1/2 weeks ago that my wife Doris and I had attended the school's teacher/parent meeting to discuss how Brandon was doing in school. It was during this meeting that Brandon's teacher had informed us that Brandon was a wonderful student because he worked well with his teachers and peers. We also learned from the teacher that he had a good sense of humor and he was playful with his classmates. We learned for the first time that Brandon had developed a friendship with his physical education teacher. We were not surprised to hear his teacher's positive evaluation of him because we had observed his classroom interactions in his previous schools, which were also positive. In fact, Brandon's interest in nature and music had won him many friends at the schools he had attended. We were also interested to meet Brandon's new teacher, and to learn what the teacher's experience with Brandon had been that had earned his confidence. Then it was time to enter Brandon's classroom and begin the meeting with his teachers and the supply teacher that Brandon was reported to have behaved improperly towards.

I saluted Brandon's classmates and teachers, and the class responded. One of the students rushed to greet me at the door. This student was also autistic. He introduced himself to me, followed by his introduction of me to his classmates. I said "good afternoon class" and they responded "good afternoon, sir." I was astonished to see for the first time a nonverbal student courageously communicating with me through verbal expression and thanking me for visiting the class. After the introduction, the teachers took Brandon and me to the other end of the classroom. I was told that Brandon had behaved inappropriately towards one of the supply teachers. Brandon's teacher asked the supply teacher to demonstrate to those in attendance what Brandon had done to her. The teacher victim clenched a fist and hit her right hand where Brandon was supposed to have hit. Then the teacher asked about Brandon's recent behaviour at home. The first question the teacher asked was whether Brandon had been aggressive at home since we last met. I replied in the negative. In fact, I had been practising with Brandon the day before how to greet people with a handshake. We had also been practising "high fives" and "hellos". We had been working on how he should greet his teachers whenever he goes to school or his family upon his return from school. After his teacher's report of what had happened, I realized that Brandon's handshake had got him in trouble. I was worried about how the misinterpretation of his practice of a handshake might affect his socialization. How do I explain the experience to a child with autism? Or how do I explain Brandon's action? I began my testimony describing him as one of the most disciplined and well-behaved children among his siblings. It was my turn to ask Brandon his version of events. I was confronted with the task of negotiating with and engaging a child with autism who seldom verbalizes to share with us his side of the story.

He realized that the salutation skills we had been practising at home had put him in trouble. The "high fives" and "hellos" had been misinterpreted as improper behaviour. How should he explain himself? His only recourse was to challenge the idea of the behaviour expected of an autistic child, an expectation that left his behavioral differences out in the cold. He could only advocate for himself by explaining what he wanted to do as clearly as possible. This means that he had to explain his experience of the situation. One could easily sense through his expressive language that his conscience compelled him to explain himself accurately so as to get out of the situation that his learning difference had placed him in. I asked Brandon to demonstrate to the assembly how and where he had hit his teacher. I knew that if I had asked him to explain what happened without giving him the opportunity to physically demonstrate, he would have been confused.

The teachers and the school authorities were dumbfounded at how accurately Brandon demonstrated his understanding of the incident. When I invited Brandon to report on his side of the story, I could see them grabbing their chairs and pressing their backs against the wall because they thought that Brandon would not be able to demonstrate to them what really took place. I told Brandon to be calm because he would be fine. After he had calmed down, I began asking my questions.

I asked Brandon questions that I knew he could answer. I asked him to explain to us if he had hit his teacher, as his teachers had reported, to make sure that he understood the reason why we were having the meeting. Brandon replied "no" with his eyes gazing at mine. I asked him to demonstrate to us how he would hit a person who made him angry. His response was "no hitting," meaning that he would not hit anyone even if he was provoked. I decided to redirect my questions to get him to move beyond his personal ethics.

I knew that Brandon had well-developed gross motor skills such as his ability to ride tricycles and to engage in child-friendly rock climbing. I was also aware of his fine motor skills such as his ability to hold a pencil and a paper in his hands. He could draw circles and straight lines but I was not aware of whether he could clench a fist to hit his teacher or not.

I was asking a child with autism who barely knew what his demonstration would mean to his observers. I asked him to show me how to clench a fist to hit people who treated him badly. I did not know if he could clamp his hand together to strike someone. If he could, I did not know what his response would be. He respectfully agreed to cooperate by demonstrating to his audience how he would make a fist. After several efforts he was having difficulty clenching his fingers for several reasons. His underdeveloped sensory motor skills would not allow him to clench his hand to strike his teacher as had been reported. After several attempts, Brandon was unable to come up with a clenched fist. After observing that he did not have the ability to clench his hand on his own, let alone strike anyone, his teachers withdrew his suspension. The question that crisscrossed my mind was "why did the teachers get it so wrong after working with a child for several years?" Several other questions followed, as I sought to understand how the teachers had mishandled a child with autism who expresses himself differently.

Brandon's teachers should have understood his actions because they have been working with him for more than two years. The teachers' failure to recognize a student's learning differences was not, of course, limited to Brandon but their lack of knowledge about him was certainly making it hard for them to overcome his challenges.

What we all learned from the experience was that it was a rush to judgment based on insufficient information about Brandon's learning differences. The teacher's premature judgment sent conflicting messages to Brandon. Such experiences could have a negative impact on teacher/student relationships. For the first time, the teachers realized that Brandon's behaviour was atypical and could easily be misinterpreted; they also realized that he was genuinely expressing himself in a non-violent way. Understanding his self-expression was the best possible way he could have been understood. It followed that the teacher's rush to judgment has been self-serving and had the potential to undermine future teacher/learner relationships (Osei, Journal entry, 2005).

Brandon's relationship with his teachers improved over time. In grade nine, he demonstrated that he could communicate with his teachers and his needs were taken seriously. He had well-developed language skills and he could clearly differentiate between his dual languages. His personal care and social skills had improved drama- tically. He could report events that happened in school and who got into trouble with his teacher. He would report about the activities he enjoyed that day and what he expected to do the next day. In Brandon's final educational assessment before entering into grade nine, his educational examiner noted the following:

As assessment tasks were presented, Brandon required a lot of time to process information, and a variety of prompts were needed to get Brandon to initiate a task, largely due to an apparent lack of understanding. Typically, it took Brandon one trial to understand what was expected on a task, and then he was more likely to initiate responses on his own and persist in completing a task. Brandon's behaviour while completing tasks suggested an inherent sense of mastery and intrinsic moti- vation to complete tasks presented to him. Also, Brandon was very motivated by social praise in attempting, persisting with, and completing tasks, and in behaving appropriately. (Boyko, 2007, p. 5)

It is clear from the report that Brandon's teachers have had real difficulties in their attempts to help him improve his classroom work. The report recognized that Brandon needed a lot of time to process information because of his difficulty navigating between two languages. There was also the problem of addressing the behavioural excesses that stemmed from his autism disorder. These difficulties were evident in his nursery school report and they remained in his grade eight assessment report. Switching languages in particular presented difficulties for Brandon as well as his teachers. His interest in music, however, contributed immensely to the improvement in his socialization. As parents/educators, we exploited his impulsive and receptive language skills to help him overcome his language difficulties and to teach him additional social skills. Brandon's motivation to learn was also recognized in his nursery school report but his teachers' frustration at not being able to understand his expressions made it difficult for them to work with him.

SUMMARY

Making Brandon's biographical story available to his school would empower both Brandon and his teachers. The Sesame Street story provides an example of Brandon's preschool experiences and what his teachers need to know to help him improve his classroom skills. The impulses Brandon displayed were learning behaviours that teachers needed to know if they were to understand who he is and where he wants to go. We learn from Dewey that "natural impulses and desires constitute in any case the starting point" for developing social and cognitive growth (Dewey, 1939, p. 64). These experiential situations cannot be replaced with educational assessment reports because they are unique experiences that cannot be captured by behavioural assessment tools. It was difficult for Brandon to work with many of the therapists that came to his classroom because he misunderstood the plethora of information they needed from him. These experiences are cumbersome and problematic for many autistic students who have to deal with what are often for them the somewhat alien social and cultural aspects of education before they can understand what is to be learned.

As Hughes (1996) has observed, the ability to reason is key to knowing who we are and how we think of others and the world. Van Manen (1990) informs us that as parent-educators, "we are interested in pedagogic competence because we realize that it is not enough to bring children into the world and love them, or to accept a job as a teacher and to lecture about history or science" (p. 158). By learning about the pedagogic competence in Brandon's impulses as a parent-educator, I understood his nonverbal expression much better and I was able to positively influence his academic skills in a way Van Manen describes as "worthwhile knowing and becoming" (p. 158). Brandon's impulses and our parental responses expressed the pedagogic essence of parenting as a teaching experience. In educational circles, however, there is no consensus as to how educators can engage with impulsive communication as a pedagogic function for the purpose of transforming the educational experiences of students with autism.

DISCUSSIONS AND INTERPRETATION OF FINDINGS

A conversation is not just a personal relation between two or more people who are involved in the conversation. A conversation may start off as a mere chat, and in fact this is usually the way that conversations come into being. But then, when gradually a certain topic of mutual interest emerges, and the speakers become in a sense animated by the notion to which they are now both oriented, a true conversation comes into being. (Van Manen, 1990, p. 98)

In the previous chapters of this dissertation, I discussed my fathering experience with regard to the influence of nature and music on Brandon's learning. In this chapter, while I report on the phenomenological descriptions in the course of this study, I also outline the important aspects of conducting father research. My fathering experience applies solely to my lived experience. This study in no way attempts to generalize its experiential findings and apply them to others. Any suggestion that the experience gained from this study can be applied to the experiences of others is beyond the scope of this study.

In this chapter, I explore my interactions with Brandon that began long before this study started. I discuss the various aspects of our conversations, reading sessions and engagement in outdoor activities. I discuss how our communications often began as informal chats but then Brandon increasingly led the conversation to the activities he wanted to know more about. Gradually, I learned from our interactions that nature- based learning and naturally occurring activities such as interacting with birds, birdsongs, and listening to music, were educational experiences that mattered to him. Over time, I was convinced that Brandon learns through birds, birdsongs, and music. I was motivated to follow his interactions as they provided clues for understanding who he is and how he learns.

I divide this chapter into two sections for the purpose of discussing and interpreting the phenomenological findings in this study. I reveal ways in which this study has brought insights into how Brandon socializes and learns through the process. In the first section of this chapter, I discuss my story as a graduate student and a father, who, after trying unsuccessfully to find a practical way for helping Brandon to improve his social and intellectual skills, found father research an appropriate medium of communication for acquiring the requisite information for helping Brandon to develop his social and learning abilities. In the second section of this study, I discuss "ecopedagogy" as a way of knowing, and how through father research this field study revealed Brandon's exceptional learning abilities as expressed through nature and subsequently music.

In this chapter, I identify ecopedagogy as a learning experience that guided this study. Ecopedagogy focuses on maintaining a strong pedagogical relationship without our experiences in nature and how they have been lived. I discuss how I gained knowledge in this field of study by developing a generalized approach to nature, and learning to address Brandon's educational challenges. While ecopedagogy generally discusses the fusing of the diverse teaching and learning concepts and practices in nature to promote ecological literacy, in this study it facilitated an understanding of Brandon's unique nature learning abilities. I hope also to show how experience contributes to studies in autism.

A REFLECTION ON FATHER RESEARCH

Hawkins (1682), Head (1997), and Turner and Freedman's (2004) ideas of nature and music provided a temporal space for conducting this study. According to these authors, human interest in music is influenced by nature and nature and music help people to learn. The conceptual argument has led to the examination of Brandon's interest in nature and music using father research. The information developed so far explains the influence of nature and music on Brandon's learning experience. For example, Head argues that music originates from birdsongs and birdsongs inform music. Head's argument connects birdsongs to music but it does not explain why Brandon is interested in birdsongs and music. There is an information gap in this conceptual argument and that is: what is my experience of the influence of nature and music on Brandon's learning? In order to address this important question, this study has been conducted along phenomenological research principles but in the context of father research.

The experiential story following this subsection in this chapter comes from my 1997–2003 journal, graduate work and field texts. As a graduate student and a father, I have always been fascinated with father research. This is because the focus on fathers as integral and essential members of the parenting team has recently become more popular. However, the amount of research on fathers and fathering is sparse compared to studies on mothers and mothering (Sidebotham, 2003; Boyd, 1985). I have therefore been asking myself the following questions: what constitutes father research and why have so few fathers written about their experiences with their children?

The opportunity to study my fathering experience with my own child came in 1998, one year after Brandon was diagnosed with GDD and PDD. For the first time, I learned from his assessment report that he had developmental difficulties in areas such as socializing, learning, and speaking (Handley-Derry, 2002). The diagnosis presented a serious challenge to me and put into question his education. Faced with the complexity of GDD and PDD and the difficulties he would confront in school, I was compelled to help him develop in the best way I could. A number of experts on ASD suggested a variety of treatment packages, which included medications and educational interventions aimed at helping him improve his behaviour. Most of the experts' plans failed to improve his situation.

At first, I was not sure what to do for a child I love dearly. Brandon was five, and he had started junior kindergarten and I was concerned how his social and academic difficulties would influence his education. After several visits to his specialists, his situation failed to improve; it did, in fact, get worse. He was not verbal and could not engage in a meaningful conversation. As a result, he could not be toilet-trained. He also could not engage his peers in any meaningful social activity and he showed little interest in his learning environment. It was difficult to understand what activities interested him and to engage him accordingly. Doris and I were advised by his behaviour specialists to put him on medication and visual coaching. We followed the experts' advice and he was put on medication and virtual coaching for seven years but his situation did not improve.

As a father and a graduate student who is caring for a child with autism, I did not possess adequate experience about how to help Brandon to improve his behaviour. As has been discussed in preceding chapters, my experience of farm life has positively informed my fathering practice but it was inadequate for addressing the needs and expectations of a child with autism. The difficult challenge presented me with complex choices. It left me in a state of confusion. The dearth of information on autism put me into an unsettling position in my effort to understand Brandon's social and learning needs. The difficult situation compelled me to engage in a relentless examination of my role as a father caring for a child with autism. My state of mind is reflected in a memo I wrote to myself in September 2002, at the beginning of my graduate studies at OISE/UT: "Throughout my fathering interactions with Brandon many creative expert ideas have emerged but none of the information seems to be working. What other ideas are left to pursue?" (Osei, Journal entry, 2002).

The first two years of my graduate studies was a period of transition. I decided to focus my graduate work on Brandon's development and to explore ways for helping him to improve his learning skills. I enrolled in courses that offered me the opportunity to connect my past experience to my classroom work and to help me develop information that would help me as a graduate student and a father to ultimately help Brandon to acquire productive learning skills. For the first time, I was able to discuss my fathering experience with my peers as part of my course work and to get their feedback. Without a doubt, I realized that my graduate work had given me a clear sense of self, and the requisite information to pursue the study of fathering experience with autism through father research.

A REFLECTION ON MY GRADUATE EXPERIENCE AND FATHER RESEARCH

My collection of data on Brandon's learning experience started long before this study began. Choice to study my experience of the influence of nature and music on Brandon's learning as the focus of my dissertation illustrates how important I believe the information I have discovered about this subject. My investigation of Brandon's educational experience in the past 15 years suggests that I have engaged in an inquiry into the phenomenon of fathering a child with autism as a critical self-study in which I have gained an extraordinary experience that may not have been possible if I had dealt with the material from the outside.

My graduate study offered me the opportunity to engage in continuous learning and I was able to access some of the most advanced information in the autism education field. My responsibility as father has also contributed immensely to the study. This process of engagement has been emotionally demanding because I have discovered from this study the only way to be able to address Brandon's needs is to learn with him. Our collaborative learning has also motivated me to pursue information that would help me to understand Brandon's learning skills better and make me able to help others in a similar situation. My academic and fathering experiences with autism have adequately prepared me to pursue this study. I have found the tools I never anticipated finding with which to conduct this study. Nevertheless, not one day passes without my engaging in self-doubt about the adequacy of my experience relative to Brandon's learning experience. While I recognized that active parenting offers rewards, I am also aware that fathering autism is muddled up in self-doubts because of the sparse information on autism, which makes autism parenting one of the most difficult works in human experience. Now let me take the reader through the process by which this study has been able to gain valuable information on Brandon's interest in nature and music learning beyond where it originally started.

In this study, personal narratives have been the primary source for generating and collecting field text notes and making meaning of them. Over the past decade, a variety of data collection methods have been used to measure variables in father research (Boyd, 1985). Narrative experience has been one of the most important resources in this study. As a father and a researcher, the nature of the study has made me part of the events under study. My participation helps support the veracity of the field texts.

The experience with my own father has been a lifelong project that has been continuously reconstructed by the new experiences in my fathering practice. My father narratives have likewise accounted for my own emerging fatherhood. In this complex, interconnected relationship, I am informed by my past experiences that help to inform my relationship with Brandon.

FATHER RESEARCH: STORIES OF EXPERIENCE

Studies have revealed that the form of data collection in many early father researches has been problematic because researchers emphasized mothers as the primary means for collecting field text (Boyd, 1985). Designating fathers as being primarily responsible for providing for the family and a subsequent lack of focus on fathers as caretakers of their children, has contributed to the sparse information on father research. In this study, I found my fathering stories to be a transformative experience that enabled me to reflect on my past experiences, and progress towards a new experience of self. In many ways, father research has helped me to find my voice in my stories by offering this study a narrative link between myself and my relationship to others and the world. In Fullagar and Owler's (1998) observation, we learn that:

Stories as the vehicles of imagination enable us to move towards a different experience of self. Just as significantly, leisure experiences offer opportunities to imagine our desires and thus recreate our sense of who we are. The stories we tell about our last holiday or the weekly game of sport whether watched or played, provide the narrative link between our past and future self, as well as between ourselves and others. In telling such stories we have the opportunity of producing a sense of ourselves as a unique person which can create a feeling of positive difference. (Fullagar & Owler, 1998, p. 446)

My experience with father research in many ways reflects the concept that stories represent our lives. We learn from Fullagar and Owler that in telling our stories we share what we know about ourselves. As a father researcher in this study, I see myself as a narrative subject through my perceptions, feelings, thoughts, and actions in relation to Brandon's learning experience. As a graduate student as well, my academic work relates to Brandon's educational development and provides me with the tools to pursue this study. Father research also provides me with a narrative link to the past, and in so doing, helps me to understand who I am as a father and my role as a father researcher in this study.

THE INNER NARRATIVE AND FATHER RESEARCH

About two years ago, during the course of this study, I had the opportunity to present my story in front of graduate students, parents, and educators at the Eighth Annual Graduate Student Research Conference of the Department of Sociology and Equity Studies in Education, OISE/UT. As I shared my story entitled, "My Experience of the Influence of Nature and Music on Brandon's Learning", I gained an in-depth understanding of my knowledge of Brandon's learning experience in a way no one else could have unless they were me. The experience encouraged the development of this study. Discussing my experience in this study, I have been able to connect with my past and current experiences to plan for the future. In the next section of this chapter, I discuss ecopedagogy as a family's shared narrative of identity that transformed a father's practical knowledge. I elaborate on how ecopedagogy helped me as a father to develop a personal curriculum for parenting a child with autism. I highlight some of our important experiences with nature and music in the context of schooling. I discuss the multiple identities that Brandon found in nature and music learning that helped prepare him for learning new skills. The information developed in this study should help prepare educators to develop appropriate curricular experiences to meet the needs and interests of children with autism.

A FAMILY SHARED NARRATIVE OF IDENTITY

One of the most important experiences revealed in this study is the discovery of a family shared narrative of identity, one that has motivated our family to learn about who we are and what we can become. Sacks (1985) observed that the stories we tell about ourselves reveal to us a sense of who we are. Fullargar and Owler (1998) share this experience in their assertion that our personal narratives are the basis of our identity and inform our actions. We also learn from Van Manen (1990) that stories are schools for transitions and transformations.

During my deliberations in this study, I discovered that my family's stories had schooled me in extraordinary ways by helping me to develop a comprehensive understanding of my fathering role through the experience of a child living with autism. I have also discovered in this study how Brandon's interest in nature has helped to improve my own ways of learning and made it easier for me to address his learning needs. Gadotti (2000) and Jardine (2000) conceptualize this sense of self as ecopedagogy. My sense of ecopedagogy (see Glossary) brought new meaning to my fathering identity after I learned that Brandon had autism. The experience compelled me to reflect on my own experience with nature and nature education. In my reflection, I learned how nature and nature education had transformed my experiences and helped fix my sense of identity.

In this study, I found that ecopedagogy works because it taught me love, care, creativity, patience, inspiration, and how to acquire new information in the process of fathering a child with autism. The new sense of self inspired me to encourage Brandon to explore the park and listen to the birds mimic sounds to him. Over time I found that our interactions in the park had inspired Brandon to learn songs he could sing to the birds. For example, the Lady in red by Chris De Burgh (1986) was the first song I heard him sing. It was this same song he first learned to dance along with. From my observations, I found that Brandon's interest in birds had inspired his confidence, creativity, and his ability to learn songs. He likes to sing to the birds.

Eventually, I realized that his relationship with birds and music is explained by Hawkins' (1682), Head's (1997), Turner and Freedman's (2004) concept of nature and music. According to the authors, nature inspires music, and nature and music motivate people to learn. The link between nature and music told me that Brandon was learning something unique.

While Brandon was developing friendships within the bird community in the park, he was also learning through the birds. After a while, I observed that Brandon's social and intellectual difficulties had ameliorated because of his engagement with the birds in the park. My experience was supported by Boyko's (2007) assessment report that "Behaviourally, the classroom teacher reported that Brandon seems to have become better at controlling his behaviour this school year and is much easier to redirect than previously." Brandon's socialization with the birds was generating positive results. His interest in learning about the ecology of birds had expanded his word vocabulary and he could communicate in meaningful sentences in grade eight. Boyko describes Brandon's progress in grade eight as satisfactory. She observes that "Current assessment results indicated that Brandon's overall cognitive functioning was in the moderately delayed range. The same was true of both his verbal and nonverbal cognitive skills. Relative cognitive strengths for Brandon included his quantitative reasoning and working memory skills." This was the first time that Brandon's diagnoses of GDD and PDD have been evaluated and downgraded to mild autism.

The report was encouraging because living in a culture which has historically valued functioning social and cognitive abilities as indicating normality, it was hopeful to discover that Brandon's interactions with birds were helping him to lessen his social and learning differences. I realized that without his exposure to the birds in the park, he might not have been able to improve his social and learning skills. For example, Fullargan and Owler have observed that rational intelligence is a measure of progress in society and children considered as lacking in rational intelligence are subjected to discrimination (Fullargan & Owler, 1998). I discovered through this study that intelligence comes in many ways. Brandon found his ways of knowing and doing through his interaction with birds, birdsongs, and music. This domain of knowledge has not been adequately explored for its contribution to the education of children with autism. Exploring this realm of education can help special education researchers to advance the education of children with autism beyond discourses of therapy to the teaching domain where students living with autism and their teachers can engage in creative and productive ways of learning. Such collaborative engagement can help to improve the relationship between teachers and children living with autism spectrum disorders.

In the stories that follow, I elaborate on my understanding of my experience of the influence of nature and music on Brandon's learning, which I have learned through the process of conducting this study. I discuss my role as a father and a research participant within father research. I elaborate on how this study helped me to discover Brandon's social and intellectual abilities. I draw connections between the findings of this study, the data and information collected, the phenomenological research literature, and notions of nature and music learning discussed herein. The phenomenological description of Brandon's interactions with birds and birdsongs provide constructive and distinctive field texts on the educational experience of a child with autism, which may not have been otherwise possible in autism education studies.

THE SESAME STREET STORY

The Sesame Street television program is one of the most educational activities that I have enjoyed with Brandon. It is his favourite television program. The stories introduced Brandon to educational activities to help him prepare for school. The televised program consisted of indoor and outdoor learning. The indoor activity focused on activities such as lettering, reading, counting, and house cleaning. The outdoor lessons include learning about animal life, weather conditions, crossing the street, and developing social skills. Even after 15 years of watching it, Sesame Street remains Brandon's most popular educational and entertainment program.

As a graduate student, my primary interest was to examine Brandon's expressions during our watching of the Sesame Street segments. As has been discussed in Chapter Six, the stories offered Brandon the opportunity to learn about animals, multicultural experiences, music, and basic life skills. He responded to the experiences in the televised stories by expressing himself in exceptional ways that were important for the development of this study. As a father, the televised segments helped me to acquire information that was useful for understanding my role in Brandon's learning experience.

One morning, after breakfast, Brandon asked me if he could watch the Sesame Street episode entitled "Journey to Ernie." I answered, "Yes, you can." I asked him if I could watch the show with him. He replied affirmatively. As we sat on the couch, enjoying the story, we saw Ernie hide inside a box with a striped pattern similar to that of his shirt. Ernie had to find where Big Bird was hiding. After Ernie searched a few boxes he finally found Big Bird. Brandon was heartbroken that Big Bird was found; he was unhappy and as a result did not cheer Ernie.

One segment began with Big Bird's attempt to find Ernie's hideout (the animated environment changes, and Big Bird no longer hides in a box). Big Bird is now looking for Ernie based on the hints Ernie had used to find him. When Big Bird was about to find Ernie, I heard Brandon shout out loudly, "eeeeeee, deeeee," meaning that Ernie is there. When Big Bird finally found Ernie, I observed him heave a sigh of relief. I saw him smiling and clapping his hands, and at the same time he was using gestures to communicate his support for Big Bird. Brandon's spontaneous response to Big Bird's successful search demonstrated his preference for Big Bird.

The episode revealed important information for this study. Brandon's under-standing of the television episode revealed his preference for learning through birds. Another important discovery was his attentive listening skill during the televised segment. In his nursery school reports, his teachers complained about the difficulty he had in staying on task. I found that when home activities are developed around birds, Brandon learns. Big Bird and Ernie's closing song may have also contributed to Brandon's interest in music.

CONNECTIONS TO ZOO

One of the most important influences in Brandon's educational development is his experiences at the zoo. Brandon's interest in birds and birdsongs encouraged me to explore the influence of his zoo interactions on his learning skills. His interactions with animals in the zoo generated important information for developing this study.

Brandon revealed his interest in birds and birdsongs in the first three months of his life. My experience of the important role that birds and birdsongs played in addressing his emotional difficulties encouraged me to explore his relationship with animal sounds. His fascination with birds and birdsongs compelled me to ask the question, "Where did Brandon's interest in birds and birdsongs originate?" My attempt to address the question motivated me to introduce him to the rhythmic sounds of frogs and to observe whether he would react in a way similar to how he reacts to birds and birdsongs. The best place to study Brandon's relationship with animal sound was the zoo. During this study several important bits of information were discovered that were relevant to Brandon's educational development.

In Brandon's zoo visits, he demonstrated his interest in learning through animals he was fascinated about. The zoo offered a variety of animal species along, of course, with the sounds they make. During my observations of his interactions with the animals in the zoo, I discovered that in addition to birds, Brandon likes to interact with frogs. The frog calls puzzled him because he pointed at a mountain frog repeatedly and he looked as if he had a question on his mind. I was stunned when I heard him mimic the sounds of the frogs back to the frog. His demonstration of an attentive listening skill during his learning experience in the zoo suggested that he was experiencing something unique.

It was observed that animal behaviour influenced Brandon in extraordinary ways. For example, Brandon was motivated to learn how to bathe himself when he saw an elephant throw water on her back. He asked me what the elephant was doing and I replied that it was having a shower. The experience had a positive impact on Brandon because whenever I was about to bathe him he would ask me to allow him to bathe by himself. I knew that his experience with the elephant had had a positive impression on him. At this point, I was convinced that Brandon had an interest in learning through animals he likes.

Brandon's interest in animal and plant ecology advanced after his visits to the zoo. He expressed interest in having his own garden because he wanted to grow food crops to feed the animals he liked (birds, camels, elephants, and frogs). His mentioning of "farm, farm, farm" indicated that he understood what a farm was and he was ready to develop one he could call his own.

The penguins also motivated us to develop a new interest in movies that featured animals. The March of the Penguins convinced Brandon to watch movies about animal life. For a child who has limited social interests, his new interest in watching movies featuring animals he likes was an important discovery and a major breakthrough in his learning experience.

SELF-ADVOCACY

At age four, Brandon's interest in birds, birdsongs and music had advanced. His interaction with birds advanced from mere observation to a sense of curiosity. He had acquired knowledge of bird sounds and he learned how to mimic the sound back to the birds. Mimicking sounds became a way of communicating with the birds. He enjoyed the sounds of the birds, and from the bird sounds he learned songs he could sing. He also learned to dance, socialize, and cognitively engage the birds in musical activity. He would sing to the birds and the birds would mimic the sound back to him. He approached the birds qualitatively because his experience with birds went far beyond socialization; he sought to rehabilitate himself as a progressive learner.

I learned in this study that the natural landscape has often been presented to children with autism and other neurological related disorders, through discourses of 'therapy' (Louv, 2006; 2008). My observation of Brandon's interaction with the birds challenges such a construct. In fact, I began this study with a preconceived idea that bird play could act as a therapy for addressing Brandon's social and cognitive challenges. However, his interactive spirit and consistent engagement with birds indicated to me that he had found his vocation for transforming his social and learning skills. I observed Brandon's learning zeal in a way that challenged me to improve my own parent/educator role in his educational development. For the first time, I decided to put him in charge of his learning environment by allowing him to make decisions relative to what he wanted to do. For example, he could sing whatever song he wanted to sing and engage in an activity of his choosing. I observed that the learning environment was an indicator of what type of songs he selects and sings. At one point, I heard him sing Celine Dion's song, "Because you loved me" to the birds.

Without a doubt, Brandon's desire to learn songs, his ability to sing, dance, and engage birds intellectually were more than an idle entanglement. They indicated a sense of emotion and empathy for the birds that flew around him. His connection with birds has generated many social and learning opportunities. In fact, a recent assessment of his speech and language pathology indicated that his outdoor activities had contributed immensely to improving his speech and language development (Nesterenko, 2008).

Recent studies on nature have produced different objectives and methods of engagement for children with autism. For example, Graettinger (2008) argues for the engagement of autistic students in natural environments that can be places for leisure and relaxation. On the other hand, Jackson (2006) and Louv (2006; 2008) point to the importance of encouraging autistic children and those with other impairments, to utilize natural places as therapeutic sites. Brandon's interaction with the birds indicated to me something different. Birds and birdsongs serve as pedagogic sites for Brandon to learn to be able to self-advocate for the things that matter to him.

Music has been one of Brandon's most preferred social and learning activities throughout his schooling. He began singing songs before he reached age two and he learned to dance to rhythm when he turned six. This means that he learned to sing before he could speak. Woodward and Hogenboom (2002) have observed that it is common for autistic children to show an interest in music before they are able to speak. Many music educators have made the effort to help children with autism increase their social and intellectual skills through music. Cohen (1998) and Exkorn (2005) introduced music as an effective therapy for improving behavioral differences among children with autism. Within such a therapeutic construct, music is rationalized as an activity designed to occupy time and space. Music is considered simply as a means to manage autistic children's undesirable behaviours. The weakness in such a therapeutic model of music is the failure of educators to demonstrate how music positively influences children with autism.

My observation of Brandon's music skills during the development of this study revealed something unique. Brandon socializes and learns through music. He processes information faster when instructions are put into music through lyrics and rhythm. He learned songs because he wanted to sing to the birds. It was discovered in the study that Brandon did not consider music a therapeutic activity; music was a part of his identity. He found learning songs and singing as his vocation because they were his preferred way of socializing with others and learning new skills. Brandon's experience with birds and birdsongs encouraged him to learn songs he could sing to birds. He did not wait for music to come to him; rather he sought after music, learned music and sang songs to the birds and his peers. Unlike many autistic children who engage in music as a passive activity, he found music a medium for learning and acquiring new skills.

Brandon's ability to learn songs and sing to birds indicated his readiness to learn through birds. He demonstrated more interest in outdoor activities than in indoor play. At first, I underestimated the impact that birds in the park had had on his sense of self, but from my interactions with him, I have learned that he considers birds as a means for learning about the world. I will point to a bird and ask him to say "bird eats," or "bird flies." His interest was to feed the birds by putting corn for them into the feeder for the birds in the park to eat. His interest in nature continued and it did not fade out as he got older.

ECOPEDAGOGY: A FATHERING TOOL

The influence of nature and music on my fathering experience has been one of the most important experiences in my fathering practice. The concept of ecopedagogy in nature and nature education has helped to advance my understanding of nature beyond discourses of therapy. As discussed in the preceding chapters, Brandon and I have approached nature and nature education as sites of learning, places where we acquired new skills that strengthened our relationship.

Brandon's interest in birds and birdsongs introduced me to new realities in parenting. As a father, I realized that I could not concentrate only on my household responsibilities (feeding and housing them), but I also needed to support Brandon as he learned about himself, others and the world. His interest in nature and music has helped us to love each other more and develop a caring relationship that has advanced our individual social and intellectual abilities. The caring relationship we have developed in the course of this study has helped us to appreciate the value of family and education.

Brandon's interest in nature inspired me to be patient and learn from him as he learned from me. Our love for each other and our collective interest in nature and music has helped us to make meaning of our lives. Our caring relationship empowered us to be creative in our development as we learn more about the world. As Noddings (2005, p. 124) has observed, "Those people who work lovingly and successfully with the severely retarded usually find other forms of human response that are as valuable as reason." The loving and caring relationship Brandon and I developed made it easy for us to understand each other's laughter, smiles, hugs, eye contact, facial expression, and the ability to understand our respective needs.

Unfortunately, in many families and schools, such loving and caring relationships are absent and the harmful impact of this on children is worrisome. Developing loving and caring relationships in our interactions with children with autism spectrum disorders could contribute enormously to education by helping parents and educators to understand the diverse human expressions and responses in our interactions with people who have special needs. As Noddings has observed, knowledge for developing loving and caring relationships with people with developmental differences comes not only from texts or lectures but from our ability to understand difference and our willingness to develop loving and caring relationships with those considered different.

CONNECTIONS TO PERSONAL CARE TRAINING

In this study, developing teaching activities around Brandon's interest in birds, birdsongs and music helped him to develop toileting skills. Brandon's fascination with birds, birdsongs and music motivated us to engage him in a creative activity by taking him to the park and introducing him to how birds poo in their cages and eat from their feeders. With love and patience we were able to develop toileting training activity that was of interest to him.

As expressed in Brandon's school reports, the lack of toilet skills was preventing him from developing his social and intellectual skills and Brandon's teachers and parents were concerned. The Geneva Centre and several of Brandon's teachers suggested different training activities. The prominent activity was the visual coaching but Brandon's lack of verbal skills and the difficulty for others to communicate with him made his visual coaching difficult. I observed that Brandon's lack of interest in what others were doing and his lack of attentive listening skills made it difficult for him to learn with visual materials. I realized that if Brandon could find an activity that he was interested in and if I could work with him around his interest, we might be successful in coaching him visually.

Brandon's teachers adored him and they enjoyed having him in their classroom. His teachers worked hard to help him to acquire the requisite classroom skills to improve his academic and social performances. Brandon was fortunate to have teachers who were enthusiastic and ready to support his success in school. He enjoyed working with his teachers because they were committed to their work. The teachers liked playing tickling games with him. His teachers observed that "Brandon very much enjoys hugs and physical contact. He is extremely ticklish," (Dobbin, Johnson & McNeil, 1997, p. 1). The teachers' support for Brandon played an important role in his educational development.

His teachers believed that Brandon's lack of toileting skills was negatively impacting his classroom performance. A teacher report by Dobbin, Johnson and McNeil (1997) states that Brandon's difficulty in developing toileting skills has made it harder for him to socialize and learn with his peers. His lack of progress in toilet use contributed to his teachers' frustration and the classroom emotions were communicated in his teacher reports. Teacher frustration was not outwardly directed at Brandon but the felt lack of classroom support and preparation were having their impact on Brandon's relationship with his teachers. According to Dobbin, Johnson and McNeil (1997), "Brandon is not yet toilet trained although it has started. He will occasionally sit on the toilet and from time to time pee there. He tends to have gas frequently and sometimes cries possibly with gas pains. Bowel movements tend to be very loose, soft with a very strong odour" (Dobbin, Johnson and McNeil (1997, p. 1). The question is: How do you help a child with autism to develop toileting skills?

Musing over how to help Brandon develop toileting skills, and not knowing what to do, I turned to the birds in the park for ideas to help me develop this activity that I believed would convince Brandon to learn the skills himself. Brandon's behaviour with the birds was positive because he was always happy and his energy was high when he was with them. His exuberance provided a clue to the role birds could play in his toilet use training. Developing toileting activities around birds not only motivated him to learn but it challenged him; if birds could poo in their cages, then he could also poo in the toilet bowl. Drawing his attention to the birds and knowing that the birds expected him to use the toilet bowl encouraged him to learn because he did not want to lose his friendship with the birds.

I discovered that I could take Brandon to the park and develop toileting skills training activity with him using birds as pedagogic tools. I introduced the idea of a cage to Brandon as a bird's private space where toileting activities take place. I described a feeder to Brandon as a bird's dining area. Brandon liked the symbols and demonstrations because they were about the birds he cared very much about. After coaching him continuously for 45 minutes, I decided to take him to see if he would remember the activity.

When the time came for Brandon to use the washroom, I invited him to where the stage has been prepared for his toileting debut. I asked him to sit on the toilet bowl but he resisted. I then reminded him to poo like the bald eagle had done in the cage. It worked for the first time and he was happy because he had successfully poohed in the toilet bowl. I was worried about his initial resistance and as a result, I decided to put the toileting instructions into a theme song and sing to him to remind him that he always has to poo in the toilet bowl. The following day, he went to the washroom and poohed in the toilet bowl as he had been instructed to do the day before. Since then, he would say to me, "Brandon poos like the birds." Brandon's achievement was amazing because he learned through birds. In fact, using the birds as a coaching tool was an activity I imagined and constructed. I was not sure if the activity would work for a child with autism but it did.

When Brandon went to school the next day he told his teachers that "Brandon poohed in the toilet bowl" His teachers were ecstatic and they congratulated him for his effort. His lack of toilet training skills has been an impediment in his educational development. In fact, his difficulty in developing personal care skills such as toileting ethics has prevented him from socializing with his peers. I informed his teachers how we learned using birding activity. When the time came for Brandon to use the toilet in school, he told his teachers that "Brandon poos in the toilet bowl," meaning that he wanted to use the washroom.

SUMMARY

In conclusion, one of the most important contributions to Brandon's educational development has been our ability to develop a loving and a caring relationship with him. Our willingness to learn from him as he tried to learn from us has produced many important benefits. Brandon's relationship with birds and birdsongs helped the study to discover many important areas in his social interaction and learning skills that might not have been possible if we had not followed his interest in birds and birdsongs when his fascination with birds first revealed itself. Our relationship with Brandon has helped us to understand the challenge autism poses to education and how following a child's interest could make a difference in the education of children with autism. For Brandon, whenever he was anxious or confused, it was his interest in nature and music that led us to find an appropriate activity to address his social and learning needs.

Unfortunately, developing loving, patience, understanding, and caring relationships in the education of students with autism spectrum disorders have been lacking in many schools. Such relationships are important for developing trust between students with autism and their educators. Students' distrust for their educators will ultimately deprive teachers of the opportunity to get to know their students and help teachers to become progressive researchers in their classrooms. Failing to develop trust in the classroom, teachers will not be able to acquire the necessary experience to develop creative and productive relationships with their students living with autism.

SUMMARY, RECOMMENDATION, AND IMPLICATIONS

A conversation is not just a personal relation between two or more people who are involved in the conversation. A conversation may start off as a mere chat, and in fact this is usually the way that conversations come into being. But then, when gradually a certain topic of mutual interest emerges, and the speakers become in a sense animated by the notion to which they are now both oriented, a true conversation comes into being. (Van Manen, 1990, p. 98)

In the previous chapter, I discussed the knowledge that I have gained in my experience of the influence of nature and music on Brandon's learning. I examined my interactions with Brandon that began long before this study started. I elaborated on the various aspects of our conversations, reading sessions and our engagement in outdoor activities that began as informal leisure activities, but with Brandon increasingly leading the communication to the things he wanted to know more about. Gradually, I learned from our experience that nature-based learning and naturally occurring activities such as interacting with birds, birdsongs, and listening to music, were activities that he enjoyed. Over time, I was convinced that Brandon learns through birds, birdsongs, and music. I was motivated to follow his interest in birds, birdsongs, and music because they provided a clue for understanding who he is and what he wants to become.

I divide this chapter into three sections to help me focus on the overall significance of this study. In this chapter, I draw attention to our own experiences and related knowledge that I explore and discuss in this study in order to inform educators, parents, service agencies, professional workers, and respite programmers about how to advance the social and learning experiences of children with autism and other impairments. For example, this study may contribute to the literature on autism studies by providing a contextual understanding of autistic children's naturalistic ways of learning. The study could help to advance information about the stages of autistic children's developmental transitions and transformations in education. This part of the study is important because there is a need for information about the achievements autistic children and their families make in the course of their development. On this note, from a father's personal account, this study could help to bridge the information gap relating to the role that fathers of autistic children play in their children's educational development, information which is important for understanding autistic children's social and learning behaviours.

In the first section of this chapter, I provide an overview of the study. I discuss its significance in terms of my experience with Brandon's social interactions and learning experiences. In addition, I elaborate on the important role that father research has played in helping me to understand Brandon's needs. In the next section, I present the recommendations based on the knowledge gained in this study. In the final section, drawing from my fathering experience in autism, I discuss the implications of this study.

A SUMMARY OF THE STUDY

Studies have shown that special educators have not paid adequate attention to early childhood experiences in autism and to the development of creative and productive ways of organizing educational activities to elicit the interest of children with autism (McConnell, 2002). Studies have recommended community alternatives such as nature-based activities as important pedagogic tools for facilitating academic competence skills in early childhood education (Palmberg et al., 2000; Shepardson, 2005; Kola-Olusanya, 2005). Other studies have taken a more pragmatic approach for addressing learning differences in autism by recommending that autistic children have nature- based activities such as bird watching and horse riding as ways of improving their social and academic competencies (Louv, 2006). Other researchers have argued strongly for built curricular activities as offering the best educational opportunities for advancing autistic students' social and intellectual skills, (Lovaas, 1977; Lovaas et al., 1973; Lovaas et al., 1979). Relative to autism and the education of autistic students, there is scant information available in terms of how autistic children interact with nature.

Although this study provides information about the social and learning experiences of one autistic student's obsessive interest in nature and music learning, it advances community- based alternatives for the education of other children with autism.

Conceptual claims suggest that there is not a single pedagogic strategy nor is there any sense of agreement as to the promotion of a specific pedagogic activity for helping students with autism to improve their academic skills. In fact, to espouse the idea that there exists a specific way or a particular pedagogic activity for advancing the academic work skills of autistic students is problematic. It is essential to acknowledge this fact for several reasons. First, it is important to recognize that information leading to better social and academic outcomes for autistic students in education is an ongoing activity. It is in this sense that I approach the central question preoccupying this study: What roles have nature and music played in improving Brandon's academic work skills?

As a graduate student and a father, father research motivated me to reflect on my own experience of childhood and to draw from the experiences that helped me in times of confusion and self-doubt amid the turbulence of urban life. In this study, I discovered that for Brandon, interacting with nature and music helped him to address the confusion in his life.

Brandon's experience with autism was associated with limitations in the areas of socialization, cognitive skills, and developing language. The challenge facing us as his parents was: what do we need to do for a child who has been diagnosed with GDD and PDD so that he can learn social and academic skills after expert available strategies have failed to improve his situation? Where do I begin, as a father, to improve his expressive and receptive language skills? I found myself mired in more questions than answers. For me, the answer did not exist in conventional strategies but in father research. The complex nature of autism and related disorders forced me to reflect on the unique abilities that he brought to the father/child experience. The developmental problems made his recovery painstaking, but through parental and educational support he was gradually able to improve on key areas of his development.

In my previous discussion in this dissertation, I explained how I developed information in father research. Drawing insights from Hawkins' (1682), Head's (1997), and Turner and Freedman's (2004) conceptions of nature and music, I found meaning in my experiential stories of Brandon's learning experience. Our conversations, outdoor activities, and reading exercises helped contribute significant ideas to the development of this dissertation.

My conversations with Brandon started off as informal discussions; ideas of common interest then emerged, which galvanized us toward a shared experience. As Van Manen (1990) has suggested in the epigraph to this chapter, conversations lend themselves to a phenomenon. Conversation provided Brandon and I a learning space to rediscover who we are and what we could become. Hanson, Gutierrez, Brennan, and Zercher (1997) suggest that conversation is the key to any productive relationship. We also learn from Van Manen that conversations have a hermeneutic thrust: they are oriented to making sense and interpreting the idea that drives or stimulates the conversation (Van Manen, 2003).

Outdoor learning enriched our conversations; it gave us self- sovereignty to engage our curiosities in ways that transformed and empowered us. We found freedom in outdoor learning experiences because we felt a sense of belonging to the natural landscape. Louv asserts that outdoor learning provides ways of seeing the world. For me, outdoor learning provided a way for reflecting on the experiences of the past; in so doing, it changed me by providing me the space and time to engage in critical thinking. In the process, the outdoor experience informed my thoughts about how to analyse, verify and critically engage with school practices and policies.

Reading to Brandon about nature offered him the ability to construct a meaning from the naturally occurring activities in his environment. During the study, and in the field, I found that Brandon reacted positively to birds he frequently heard about in my readings but not to those less known to him. I realized that when I read about the ecology of the bald eagles, his behaviour towards the birds was more interactive than towards those he did not know. Kolic´-Vehovec and Bajsanski (2007) contend that reading is a medium for learning.

RECOMMENDATIONS

Based on the phenomenological information developed so far, it is possible to identify the factors that need to be considered in the organization of dialogue that aims to appeal to the interests of autistic students in early childhood learning. I recommend that the Ontario special education program be reorganized to allow autistic students the right to self-advocacy, irrespective of age. ASD and related disorders are complex, which makes it difficult to pinpoint specific pedagogies for advancing students' academic work skills. Over the last half century, studies have refused to explain how educators might organize educational activities to appeal to the academic interest of autistic students. The academic needs of individual autistic students are different and unique in ways that make it difficult for researchers and educators to come up with a specific curriculum that could be applied generally.

Brandon's interest in advocating for activities that matter to him, and to successfully advancing his academic work skills, suggest that if other autistic students in special education programs are given the chance to self-advocate for their interests and needs in education, most of them would develop successfully in school. The lack of self-advocacy for autistic students in public schools has not only impeded efforts to advance autistic students' social and intellectual skills, but it has also had a negative influence on special education teachers who teach autistic students. Students' self-advocacy should be taken seriously and their communications, whether verbal or nonverbal, need to be explored for their educational content in order to inform the special education field. At present, there is no specific way of organizing curricular activities for autistic students as a means for improving their social and academic skills.

The Ontario Ministry of Education guidelines for special educators do not encourage autistic students' self-advocacy in classroom planning because of the age restrictions enshrined in the document. Removing age limits would allow teachers to negotiate directly with students and include the information in classroom planning. Imposing age limitations restricts teachers' roles as researchers in their classrooms.

A NATIONAL AUTISM EDUCATION STRATEGY

Since Kanner identified autism in 1955, there has been a lack of information about autism and the education of autistic students (Geneva Center for Autism, 2005; Helen Tager-Flusberg et al., 2001; Elizabeth Starr et al., 2003). ASD prognoses suggest that autistic students are sick and that their sickness needs to be cured (Tanguay, 2000; Baron- Cohen et al., 1992; Brown et al., 2001; Kuoch et al., 2003; Kohler, et al., 2001). As a result, researchers have introduced several educational concepts over the last two decades to inform as well as to empower educators with tools for advancing the social and intellectual skills of autistic students. However, studies have indicated that many autistic students have experienced only nominal progress in school because current classroom programs are inadequate for educating autistic students to be creative and productive or in helping them to make a successful transition from school to work (Billington, 2006).

ASD presents serious challenges to educators because research studies have refused to identify appropriate education strategies for improving the academic skills of autistic students that could be replicated universally (Kohler et al., 2003). The very same studies suggest that suitable educational programs could improve the social and cognitive skills of autistic students and make them productive citizens (Brown et al., 2001; McConnell, 2002; Kohler et al., 2001; Odom et al., 1999). In practice, it is difficult to access information that offers specific educational strategies that would help bring about significant progress in the academic development of autistic students. It was a desire to help that motivated me as a father researcher to engage in a transformative process of developing a conversational relationship with Brandon to make it possible to learn from him as he learns from me so that we would be able to share with others our experiences.

Brandon's experiences learning from birds and birdsongs offer a new direction to autism studies and the education of autistic children. Studies have been done to provide autistic children with practical ways for advancing their academic skills but few of these studies have been able to demonstrate much progress. Evidence suggests that nature and nature learning offer children with learning impairments creative tools for advancing their learning skills (Louv, 2006). Laa and family (2008) have discovered that birds positively influence their autistic child's learning skills but there is a paucity of information about autistic children's learning experiences with birds and birdsongs in general. We learn from Kola- Olusanya (2005) that children react positively to nature learning. He argues that children's experiences with nature occur through their voluntary interactions with the natural landscape but he fails to provide evidence relative to how nature actually influences children's experiences. Studies have recognized children's positive attitudes to nature but few of these studies have provided the actual stories that children tell about their nature learning experiences. This challenge has presented conceptual difficulties for educators in accurately representing autistic children's learning experiences with nature and nature education.

In spite of the government of Canada's genuine effort to introduce a national autism education strategy, many conceptual problems remain unresolved. The problem is the failure of education researchers and practitioners to reach consensus on the conceptual approach to autism education. The problem has made it difficult for stakeholders in autism education to examine autistic children's early experiences in nature and to build on their primary experiences as a means of helping them to make a smooth transition from preschool to formal schooling. Such information could help in the development of a national autism education strategy. Children's primary experiences in nature and nature learning, when adequately explored, could be an important educational foundation for advancing autism education. Evidence suggests that nature education researchers could develop a common language that brings together individual experiences in nature and make this an integral part of a national autism education strategy.

According to the 2001 Participation and Activity Limitation Survey (PALS), many Canadian parents of children with social and cognitive impairments have observed that the schools cannot really help them (Kohen, Uppal, Guevremont & Cartwright, 2007a). The Program for International Student Assessments (PISA) offers insights into the widening gap in academic achievements between 15-year-olds of both typically developing students and students with social and cognitive impairments. The PISA report indicated that the academic achievements of students with social and cognitive impairments are below the national average and this has a negative impact on their future education or employment opportunities (Kohen, Uppal, Guevremont & Cartwright, 2007a).

The PISA report suggests that students with social and cognitive impairments in Ontario have the lowest level of literacy compared with students from other provinces. The reason may be that the student population in Ontario is more culturally diverse than any other province in the country. Most of these children have immigrated to Canada, and change, of any kind, can negatively impact all children's social and cognitive development. However, in a similar study the National Longitudinal Survey of Children and Youth (NLSCY) study found that the literacy gap could be improved if parents engage students in creative and productive preschool activities, mom and tot programs, and structured and unstructured outdoor programs which are all popular activities that parents have for their young children (Lipps & Yiptong-Avila, 1999). The NLSCY study suggests that such preschool programs could ease children's social adjustments and help their academic achievements, and in the long term help children to transition from preschool to formal schooling. In addition, the study recognizes that early childhood education programs are productive across cultures. Researchers identify early educational activities as capable of influencing early intellectual stimulation of brain development. For example, Lipps and Yiptong-Avila contend that "features of children's home environment and participation in easily implemented educational activities, such as early education programs and daily reading, when combined can have substantial effects on children's future vocabulary skills" (Lipps & Yiptong-Avila, 1999).

The reports from the Ontario Ministry of Education (2007b), the Ministers' Autism Spectrum Disorders Reference Group (2007), and the National Research Council (2001) have recommended an evidence-based instructional approach to the education of students with autism spectrum disorders because each student has the ability to learn. The reports also show that each student has his or her own way of learning. What I did not find in the reports was how students' interest in the early stages of their development could be adequately explored to understand the skills that preschoolers bring to the classroom. In my own experience, it was Brandon's interest in birds and birdsongs that offered me a starting point to work with him to acquire relevant skills for his educational development.

The collection of data on children's learning interest in the early stages of their development could help educators understand how each student learns and the skills they bring to school. The information would be very useful for educators to help children who may develop social and learning challenges in the future.

We learn from Heydon and Iannacci (2008), Swadener and Lubeck (1995) that the needs of culturally and linguistic diverse young children in schools require a new approach to education. They argue that contemporary curricula and policies operate from a "deficit-oriented view" where children are considered to exist with poor skills and knowledge (p. 20). According to the authors, the problem is promoting "segregation that creates and perpetuates a lampoon of at-risk children and their families" (p. 19). The solution for addressing this problem, they argue, is to promote structural changes in the education system to advance the equitable distribution of materials, resources, education, power, and self-sufficiency.

A national autism education strategy is an important starting point for exploring the social factors that motivate students with autism spectrum disorders to learn.

Information on students' interests starting from birth to adulthood would help educators to appreciate differences and the challenges children with autism face in school. Interest focused learning is imperative for understanding Brandon's social and cognitive difference and it is his interest in birds and birdsongs that introduced us to how he learns.

IMPLICATIONS FOR EDUCATORS, PARENTS, AND
PROFESSIONAL PROVIDERS

The stereotypes have greatly influenced societal perceptions of autism and autistic students, and these are reflected in the type of institutional approaches used to educate autistic persons in inner- city schools. For example, the Ontario special education guidelines for educators exclude autistic students younger than sixteen from participating in decision making about their educational development. Studies have not been able to advance beyond the social characterization of autistic students as permanently disabled without any chance for recovery. This bias has had a negative impact on parents, professional providers, and educators teaching autistic students, and the students themselves, in their acquiring access to special education programs. A national autism education strategy would be able to dispel incorrect information about autistic students and help educators to develop a positive attitude towards them. Autistic students in contemporary special education programs are being discriminated against because they cannot self-advocate for the things they want to know more about (Ontario Ministry of Education, 2001), a stance that is inconsistent with Freire's idea of critical education. According to Freire, autistic students deserve unimpeded access to education irrespective of their learning differences. Equity education in Freire's view should make the student an active participant in his or her educational transformation. Freire argues that "if people, as historical beings necessarily engaged with other people in a movement of inquiry, did not control that movement, it would be (and is) a violation of their humanity" (2003, p. 85). Hence, it is fair to ask whether the active participation of autistic students in their educational development would better prepare special educators to address the needs of autistic students, and in the process, reduce the cost of education and professional services to the taxpayer.

More recently, some autistic students have written about their living experiences with autism and they have been able to discuss what goes on in many autistic minds. This information provides researchers and educators with the lived experiences of people living with autism. These personal stories have offered new information that has not been adequately represented in autism studies. The stories that autistic students have written about themselves inform us that people living with autism share similar interests with typical developing people. However, their needs have generally been misunderstood. Another important breakthrough this study in parti- cular has made is the discovery of Brandon's ability to communicate with people without mediators. Learning with Brandon has brought forth new information about his ability to listen, understand, and follow instructions directed at him. For a child with autism, these skills are tools for self-advocacy.

Temple Grandin (2001) informs us that informed educators were able to help her to be productive, creative and able to express herself freely. Several autistic students have begun to write about their willingness to engage in a reciprocal communication with others but their listeners' inability to understand them has prevented others from exploring creative ways of communicating with people living with autism. For example, Grandin, (2001) and Willey (1999) have shared their experiences of living with autism. In her recent article," Teaching Tips for Children and Adults with Autism," Grandin (1995) introduces us to how well-informed teachers were able to engage her in meaningful communication. Her ability to engage in meaningful communication not only advanced her classroom performance, but saved her school from misusing their time and resources on activities that could best be handled by teachers with parental support. My own experiences from this study indicate that my active involvement in Brandon's schooling has probably helped his teachers to have a clearer understanding of his behaviour.

Grandin has observed that allowing autistic students to express themselves freely would help to provide information for developing educational instructions for educators working with students with autism. For example, Grandin's teachers observed that Grandin learns best when classroom activities are communicated through pictures. According to Grandin, her teachers supported her learning from pictures. What we learn here undermines current models of autism studies that characterize each autistic student's behaviour as antisocial and lacking cognitive competence. The observation has been confirmed by several autistic students who have shared with the typical developing world their experiences living with autism. The recent proliferation of student work advanced by autistic students has helped educators to address some of the unique challenges in educating autistic students. For example, Wiley explains that normalizing behavioural differences in autism is, after all, not beyond a teacher's domain. (Willey, 1999). She asserts that an informed teacher would pay adequate attention to students' interests and develop classroom activities to expand those interests. Willey (1999) contends that teaching an autistic student normal academic skills and appropriate behaviour are all about how the teacher understands the student's interest. Willey shares her experience about how her educators helped her to develop social and cognitive skills. Like Grandin, she credits teachers who knew how to solicit her interest in education. Willey describes her dialogic experiences as follows:

> Typically, my teachers took it upon themselves to analyse this pedantic behaviour of mine and I am told their fondest memories of me included adjectives like obstinate, disobedient and everyone's favourite, mentally retarded. Because my parents were learning how to talk to me, it never occurred to them that I was not following other people's directions. They knew how to get my attention, usually by allowing me the freedom to find my own way of expressing my interest. If I wanted to chew the same piece of gum for days on end, that was fine. If I wanted to shape my mouth into letters they were forming while I spoke, that was okay. If I insisted on reading my books out loud that was okay too, even if we were in the library. They knew I had my own way of doing things, and they didn't interfere with my methods

so long as the effort was genuine and the result positive. I had control of my learning environment at home and because I was so academically gifted, my parents saw no reason to interfere with a good thing. But at school, the rules changed. Suddenly, I was expected to comply with agendas and schedules that were stifling and illogical. (Willey, 1999, p. 22)

Here, we learn about the importance of practising self-sovereignty in education. Gabel (2002) for example, has discussed the importance of allowing students with diverse abilities to have equitable access to education. Grandin and Willey argue that learning by doing offered them great opportunities. In contrast, ABA prevents autistic students and other students with impairments from practising self-advocacy in education. The problem is that assistive technologies are not equipped with information about the problems they are directed to fix or they do not adequately understand the expectations of those directing them. These educational experiences from autistic people inform us that autistic students are capable of advocating for themselves and studies conducted so far demonstrate that contemporary education programs should be improved to accept autistic students as conscious and able beings and engage them as equal partners in education. Educators must be encouraged not to underestimate the social and intellectual potential of students with autism and to treat them fairly. Grandin and Willey's experiences are shared by many other autistic students. These stories confirm the understanding that dialogue lies at the heart of the education of autistic students and it is imperative that educators engage these students as equal participants in the development of their education.

SCENARIOS FOR FUTURE STUDIES

Future studies on early childhood experiences are important because they can provide an understanding of autistic students' interests and needs in education. The information about autistic students is needed if we are to understand how to engage them in creative and productive ways. Studying autistic students' early childhood experiences would go a long way to providing educators with productive information about how autistic students should be engaged in school. There should be a centralized information system that is continuously updated for special educators to inform them about the lived experiences of students with autism. This centralized information resource would provide information relating to a student's social and cognitive needs. At present, special education programs do not have in place inform-ation banks that connect students' early experiences to the future. In other words, the Ontario Students Record file (OSR) and the independent education plans (IEPs) are inadequate for providing special educators with information needed to advance the education of students with autism.

SUMMARY

Brandon's experience in education informs us that he has a unique way of learning. His learning differences correlate with the experiences of many autistic students in education. The challenge for autism studies is to challenge the implied conceptual discord characterizing those described as "learner disabled" or "learner able." According to Gabel (2002), learner disabled is a social construct resulting from discrimination toward people with difference and not really a description of an innate deficit. We learn from Sinclair (2004) that "the models of social deficit often employed to depict autistic children are themselves impaired in their ability to conceptualise individual experience. I believe in differences in autism rather than disability in autism." Studies have identified this lack of understanding on the part of educators and professional providers as a barrier to creatively engaging autistic students in a way that makes it possible to understand their needs. For example, Hobson believes that "autism studies invite some fundamental considerations about the ways in which we all come to feel, think and learn in the world; how we make sense of our experience with autism forces us to think more deeply about what human perception, or human relations, or human intelligence, or human language, or human creativity, actually are" (2002, p. 182).

Autistic students have diverse ways of learning and it is imperative for educators to develop ways that help them to meet their needs. One of the most important ways for us as parents to meet Brandon's learning needs was to take his expressions seriously and engage him accordingly. For Brandon, developing nature literacy meant his engagement in nature-based activities that were of interest to him. He found his voice in learning through birds and birdsongs. My phenomenological experience in this study indicates that autistic students' primary interactions with nature and music offer pedagogical possibilities and are worthy of further comprehensive study.

REFERENCES

Ahlberg, M. (1998). Ecopedagogy and ecodidactics: Education for sustainable development, good environment and good life. *University of Joensuu, Bulletins of the Faculty of Education, 69.*

Ainley, M., Hidi, S., & Berndorff, D. (2002). Interest, learning, and the psychological processes that mediate their relationship. *Journal of Educational Psychology, 94,* 545–561.

Alementi, C. (2007). *Guidelines outline evaluation of children with global developmental delay. American Academy of Neurology.* Retrieved February 17, 2007, http://www.eurekalert.org/pub_releases/2003-02/aaon-goe020403.php

American Psychiatry Association. (1994). *Diagnostic and statistical manual of mental disorders (DSM-IV-TR).* Washington, DC: Author.

Ansley, R. (2002). *Brandon's individual education plan (IEP) for grade four.* Toronto, Ontario, Canada: Toronto District School Board.

Attwood, T. (2000). *Should children with an Autistic Spectrum Disorder be exempted from doing homework?* Retrieved November 30, 2008, from http://www.tonyattwood.com.au/articles/pdfs/attwood7.pdf

Attwood, T. (2008, November 30). *Voices from the edge* [Series]. Audio recording posted to http://www.tonyattwood.com.au/

Autism Society of Canada. (2007). *Autism Society of Canada supports a national autism strategy.* Retrieved January 11, 2007, from www.autismsocietycanada.ca

Austern, P. L. (1998). Nature, culture, myth, and the musician in early modern England. *Journal of the American Musicological Society, 51*(1), 1–47.

Austern, P. L. (2001). Tis nature's voice: Music, natural philosophy and education and the hidden world in seventeen-century England. In S. Clark & A. Rehding (Eds.), *Music theory and natural order from the Renaissance to the early twentieth century* (pp. 30–60). Cambridge, MA: Cambridge University Press.

Baer, D. M., & Sherman, J. (1964). Reinforcement control of generalized imitation in young children. *Journal of Experimental Child Psychology, 1,* 37–49.

Baer, D. M., Wolf, M. M., & Risely, T. R. (1968). Some dimensions of applied behavior analysis. *Journal of Applied Behavior Analysis, 1,* 91–97.

Baker, B. L. (1989). *Parent training and developmental disabilities.* Washington, DC: American Association of Mental Retardation.

Baron-Cohen, S., Allen, J., & Gillberg, C. (1992). Can autism be detected at 18 months? The needle, the haystack and the chat. *British Journal of Psychiatry, 161,* 839–943.

Bennetto, L., Pennington, B., & Rogers, S. (1996). Intact and impaired memory functions in autism. *Child Development, 67*(4), 1816–1835.

Berko-Gleason, J. (1982). Insights from child acquisition of second language loss. In R. D. Lambert & B. F. Freed (Eds.), *The loss of language skills* (pp. 13–23). Rowley, MA: Newbury House Publishers.

Bexell, S. M., Jarrett, O. S., Yan, L. L. H., Sandhaus, E. A., Zhihe, Z., & Maple, T. L. (2007). Observing panda play: Implications for zoo programming and conservation efforts. *Curator, 50*(3), 287–297.

British Institute for Brain Injured Children. (2006). *Global developmental delay.* Retrieved February 16, 2007, from http://www.Bibic.org.uk/newsite/about/conditions/gdd.htm

Billington, T. (2006). Working with autistic children and young people: Sense, experience and the challenges for services, policies and practices. *Disability & Society, 21*(1), 1–13.

Bingham, C., & Morgan, B. (2006). *First nature encyclopaedia.* New York: DK Publishing.

Biasella, S. (2008). *How to comfort a crying baby.* Retrieved June 1, 2008, from http://parenting.ivillage.com/newborn/ncrying/0,,lz_6r6b,00.html

Bizerril, M. X. A. (2004). Children's perception of Brazilian Cerrado landscapes and biodiversity. *The Journal of Environmental Education, 35*(4), 47–58.

REFERENCES

Bondy, A., & Frost, L. (2001). The picture exchange communication system. *Behaviour Modification*, *25*(5), 725–744.

Boutheina, J., Mottron, L., & Dawson, M. (2006). Impaired face processing in autism: Fact or artifact? *Journal of Autism and Developmental Disorders*, *36*(1), 91–106.

Bowers, C. (2001). *Educating for eco-justice and community*. Athens, GA: University of Georgia.

Boyd, S. T. (1985). Father research: Methods. *American Behavioral Scientist*, *29*(1), 112–128.

Boyko, K. (2007). *Psychological assessment report*. Newmarket, Ontario, Canada: York Region District School Board.

Briseño-Garzón, A., Anderson, D., & Anderson, A. (2007). Adult learning experiences from an aquarium visit: The role of social interactions in family groups. *Curator*, *50*(3), 299–318.

Bronte-Tinkew, J., & Moore, K. A. (2004). *The developing a daddy survey (DADS) project: Framework paper*. Washington, DC: The National Institute of Child Health and Human Development (NICHD).

Brophy, T. (2005). A longitudinal study of selected characteristics of melodic improvisations of children ages six through twelve. *Journal of Research in Music Education*, *53*(2), 120–133.

Brown, W. H., Ragland, E. U., & Fox, J. J. (1988). Effects of group socialization procedures on the social interactions of preschool children. *Research in Developmental Disabilities*, *9*, 359–376.

Butzlaff, R. (2000). Can music be used to teach reading? *Journal of Aesthetic Education*, *34*, 3–4.

Burnard, P. (2000). How children ascribe meaning to improvisation and composition: Rethinking pedagogy in music education. *Music Education Research*, *2*(1), 7–23.

Camilleri, J. M. (1999). Disability: A personal odyssey. *Disability and Society*, *14*(6), 845–853.

Campbell, P., & Scott-Kassner, C. (2002). *Music in childhood: From preschool through the elementary grades* (2nd ed.). New York: Schirmer Books.

Carman, K., Parker, H., & Bennet, J. (2006). *Global developmental delay*. Retrieved April 17, 2008, from http://www.Bibic.org.uk/newsite/about/conditions/gdd.htm

Carta, J., Sainato, D., & Greenwood, C. (1988). Advances in the ecological assessment of classroom instructions for young children with handicaps. In S. L. Odom & M. B. Karnes (Eds.), *Early intervention for infants and children with handicaps: An empirical base* (pp. 129–143). Baltimore: Paul H. Brookes.

Casey, K. (1996). The new narrative research in education. *Review of Research in Education*, *21*, 211–253.

Cashin, A. (2003). *A hermeneutic phenomenological study of the lived experience of parenting a child with autism*. Unpublished doctoral dissertation, University of Sydney, Sydney, Australia.

Charlop, M., Scriebman, L., & Thibodeau, M. (1985). Increasing spontaneous verbal responding in autistic children using time delay procedure. *Journal of Applied Behavior Analysis*, *18*, 155–166.

Chilcoat, G. W., & Ligon, J. A. (1998). We talk here: This is a school for talking. Participatory democracy from the classroom out into the community: How discussion was used in the Mississippi Freedom Schools. *Curriculum Inquiry*, *28*(2), 165–193.

Cole, E. (1999). *The Toronto District School Board district-wide special education assessment*. Toronto, Ontario, Canada: Ontario Ministry of Education.

Cohen, S. (1998). *Targeting autism*. Los Angeles: University of California.

Cohen, V. (1980). *The emergence of musical gestures in kindergarten children*. Unpublished doctoral dissertation, University of Illinois, Urbana.

Collins, P. H. (2000). *Black feminist thought: Knowledge, consciousness, and the politics of empowerment*. London: Routledge.

Connelly, F. M., & Clandinin, D. J. (1988). *Teachers as curriculum planners*. Toronto, Ontario, Canada: Ontario Institute of Studies in Education.

Corker, M. (1999). Differences, conflations and foundations: The limits to accurate theoretical representation of disabled people's experience? *Disability and Society*, *14*(5), 627–642.

Costa Giomi, E. (1999). The effects of three years of piano instruction on children's cognitive development. *Journal of Research in Music Education*, *3*, 198–212.

Crites, S. (1971). The narrative quality of experience. *Journal of the American Academy of Religion*, *39*(3), 291–311.

Crystal, D. (n.d.). *Prosodic systems and language acquisition*. Retrieved December 8, 2008, from http://www.davidcrystal.com/DC_articles/Linguistics53.pdf

Cunningham, M. K., Meriorg, E., & Tryssenaar, L. (2003). *Parenting in Canada*. Toronto, Ontario, Canada: Nelson.

Custodero, L. A., & Johnson-Green, E. A. (2003). Passing the cultural torch: Musical experience and musical parenting of infants. *Journal of Research in Music Education, 51*(2), 102–114.

Darwin, C. (1987). A biographical sketch of an infant. *Mind, 7*, 285–294.

Danforth, S. (1999). Pragmatism & the scientific validation of professionals practices in American special education. *Disability and Society, 14*(6), 733–751.

De Burgh, C. (Producer), & Hardiman, P. (Producer/Director). (1986). *The lady in red. From into the light album*. London: A & M Records.

Decker, J. (2000). *School support team for Brandon Osei*. Toronto, Ontario, Canada: Toronto District School Board.

Deguine, J. C. (1974). *Emperor penguin*. Brattleboro, VT: Stephen Greene.

Demmert, G. W. (2005). The influences of culture on learning and assessment among Native American students. *Learning Disabilities Research & Practice, 20*(1), 16–23.

Dempsey, I., & Foreman, P. (2001). A review of educational approaches for individuals with autism. *International Journal of Disability, Development and Education, 48*(1), 103–116.

Dennard, D., & Boles, T. (1993). *Can elephant drink through their noses?* Minneapolis, MN: Carolrhoda Books.

Department of Justice of Canada. (1982). *The charter of rights and freedoms (1982)*. Retrieved April 21, 2005, from http://laws.justice.gc.ca/en/charter/

Dewey, J. (1938). *Experience and education*. New York: Macmillan.

Dewey, J. (1916). *Democracy and education*. New York: The Free Press.

Dobbin, F., Johnson, L., & McNeil, P. (1997). *Preschool teacher questionnaire*. Toronto, Ontario, Canada: Margaret Fletcher Nursery School.

Dudley-Marling, C. (2004). The social construction of learning dsabilities. *Journal of Learning Disabilities, 37*(6), 482–489.

Dyches, T. T., Wilder, L. K., Sudweeks, R. R., Obiakor, F. E., & Algozzine, B. (2004). Multicultural issues in autism. *Journal of Autism and Developmental Disorders, 34*(2), 211–222.

Dyer, K. (1989). The effects of preference on spontaneous verbal requests in individuals with autism. *Journal of the Association for Persons with Severe Handicaps, 14*(3), 184–189.

Dyson, L. L. (2003). Children with learning disabilities within the family context: Analysis with siblings in global- self concept, academic-self perception, and social competence. *Learning Disability Research and Practice, 18*(1), 1–9.

Elder, J., Valcante, G., Won, D., & Zylis R. (2003). Effects of in- home training for culturally diverse fathers of children with autism. *Issues in Mental Health Nursing, 24*, 273–295.

Exkorn, K. S. (2005). *The autism sourcebook*. New York: Regan Books.

Fabiano, G. A. (2007). Father participation in behavioral parent training for ADHD: Review and recommendations for increasing inclusion and engagement. *Journal of Family Psychology, 21*(4), 683–693.

Falk, J. H., & Dierking, L. D. (1998). Free-choice learning: An alternative term to informal learning? *Informal Learning Environments Research Newsletter, 2*(1), 2. Washington, DC: American Educational Research Association.

Federal Interagency Forum on Child and Family Statistics. (1998). *Nurturing fatherhood: Improving data and research on male fertility, family formation and fatherhood*. Washington, DC: U.S. Government Printing Office.

Fester, C. B., & DeMyer, M. K. (1961). The development of performances in autistic children in an automatically controlled environment. *Journal of Chronic Diseases, 13*, 312–345.

Flohr, J. (1985). Young children's improvisations: Emerging creative thought. *The Creative Child and Adult Quarterly, 10*(2), 79–85.

Foucault, M. (1972). *The archaeology of knowledge*. London: Tavistock.

Foucault, M. (1994). *The birth of the clinic: An archaeology of medical perception*. New York: Vintage.

REFERENCES

Freire, P. (2003). *Pedagogy of the oppressed*. New York: Continuum.
Freire, P. (1985). *The politics of education*. New York: Bergin & Garvey.
Fullagar, S., & Owler, K. (1998). Narratives of leisure: Recreating the self. *Disability and Society, 13*(3), 441–450.
Gabel, S. (2005). *Disability studies in education*. New York: Peter Lang.
Gabel, S., & Peters, S. (2004). Presage of a paradigm shift? Beyond the social model of disability toward a resistance theory of disability. *Disability and Society, 19*(6), 585–600.
Gabel, S. (2002). Some conceptual problems with critical pedagogy. *Critical Inquiry, 32*(2), 177–201.
Gadoti, M. (2000). *Pedagogy of the earth and culture of sustainability, Costa Rica 2000 Commission: A new millennium of peace*. Retrieved June 19, 2007, from http://www.earthcharter.org/resources/speeches/gado.htm
Garfinkle, A., & Schwartz, I. (1996). *Picture exchange communication system with peers: Increasing social interactions in an integrated preschool classroom*. San Francisco: The Association for Behaviour Analysis Conference.
Geneva Centre for Autism. (2005). *What is autism?* Retrieved March 13, 2005, from www.autism.net
Gibbons, G. (2008). *Green heron: Bird of mystery*. Retrieved April 17, 2008, from http://www.suite101.com/article.cfm/tropical_neotropical_birds/94236
Glesne, C. (1999). *Becoming qualitative researchers*. New York: Addison Wesley Longman.
Goode, J. (2007). Managing' disability: Early experiences of university students with disabilities. *Disability & Society, 22*(1), 35–48.
Gough, A. (1997). *Education and the environment*. Melbourne, Australia: Acer.
Graettinger, D. (2008, May 29). Calais: Autistic students leads way for nature trail. *Bangor Daily News*. Retrieved from bangordailynews.com
Grandin, T. (2001). *Teaching tips for children and adults with autism*. Retrieved May 20, 2007, from http://www.autism.org/temple/tips.html
Gray, B. (2007, April 13). Court quashes autistic kids. *Toronto Sun*, p. 26.
Grosvenor, C. (2006, January 13). *How to choose and plant apple trees*. Retrieved October 9, 2006, from http://www.howtodothings.com/home-and-garden/a2924-how-to-choose-and-plant-apple-t
Gurry, S., & Larkin, A. (1990). Daily life therapy: Its roots in the Japanese culture. *International Journal of Special Education, 5*(3), 359–369.
Halder, F. (2006). The natural environment. In R. Jackson (Ed.), *Holistic special education* (pp. 187–198). Edinburgh, Scotland: Floris Books.
Hale, C. M., & Tager-Flusberg, H. (2005). Brief report: The relationship between discourse deficits and autism symptomatology. *Journal of Autism and Developmental Disorders, 35*(4), 519–524.
Halle, J. W. (1982). Teaching functional language to the handicapped: An integrative model of natural environment teaching techniques. *Journal of the Association for the Severely Handicapped, 7*, 29–37.
Handley-Derry, M. (2002). *Brandon's developmental pediatric and behavioral analysis 1997–2002* [Letters 1–21]. Toronto, Ontario, Canada: Home Records.
Hanson, M. J., Gutierrez, S., Brennan, M. M. E. L., & Zercher, C. (1997). Language, culture, and disability: Interacting influences on preschool inclusion. *Topics in Early Childhood Special Education, 17*(3), 307–336.
Head, M. (1997). Birdsongs and the origins of music. *Journal of the Royal Musical Association, 22*(1), 1–23.
Hersen, M., & Barlow, D. H. (1976). *Single case experimental designs: Strategies for studying behavior change*. New York: Pergamon.
Hewett, F. M. (1965). Teaching speech to an autistic child through operant conditioning. *American Journal of Orthopsychiatry, 35*, 927–936.
Heydon, R., & Lannacci, L. (2008). *Early childhood curricular and the de-pathologizing of childhood*. Toronto, Ontario, Canada: University of Toronto Press.
Hidi, S., & Harackiewicz, J. M. (2000). Motivating the academically unmotivated: A critical issue for the 21st century. *Review of Educational Research, 70*, 151–179.

Hobson, P. (2002). *The cradle of thought: Exploring the origins of thinking*. London: MacMillan.

Hodge, N. (2005). Reflections on diagnosing autism spectrum disorders. *Disability & Society, 20*(3), 345–349.

Horner, R. H., Carr, E. G., Halle, J., McGee, G., Odom, S., & Wolery, M. (2005). The use of single-subject research to identity evidence-based practice in special education. *Council for Exceptional Children, 71*(2), 165–179.

Hughes, W. (1996). *Critical thinking* (2nd ed.). Peterborough, Ontario, Canada: Broadview.

Hutchison, D. (1998). *Growing up green: Education for ecological renewal*. New York: Teachers College.

Jackson, W. (2006). *How to grow carrots*. Retrieved October 9, 2006, from http://www.howtodothings. com/home-and-garden/a1804-how-to-grow-carrots.htm

Jardine, D. W. (2000). *Under the tough old stars: Ecopedagogical essays*. Brandon, VT: Solomon Press.

Jemel, B., Mottron, L., & Dawson, M. (2006). Impaired face processing in autism: Fact or artifact? *Journal of Autism and Developmental Disorders, 36*(1), 91–106.

Johnson, L., Dobbin, F., & McNeil, P. (1997). *Preschool teacher report*. Toronto, Ontario, Canada: Margaret Fletcher Daycare Centre.

Kamio, Y., Wolf, J., & Fein, D. (2006). Automatic processing of emotional faces in high-functioning pervasive developmental disorders: An affective priming study. *Journal of Autism and Developmental Disorders, 36*(2), 155–167.

Kahn, R. (2003). *Paulo Freire and eco-justice: Updating pedagogy of the oppressed for the age of ecological calamity*. Retrieved December 6, 2007, from http://www.paulofreireinstitute.org/freireonline/ volume1/1kahn1.htm

Kasari, C. (2002). Assessing change in early intervention programs for children with autism. *Journal of Autism and Developmental Disorders, 32*(5), 447–461.

Kiehn, M. T. (2003). Development of music creativity among elementary school students. *Journal of Music Education, 51*(4), 278–288.

Koegel, R. L., Dyer, K., & Bell, L. K. (1987). The influence of child preferred activities on autistic children's social behavior. *Journal of Applied Behavior Analysis, 20*, 243–252.

Koegel, R. L., O'Dell, M. C., & Koegel, L. K. (1987). A natural language teaching paradigm for non-verbal autistic children. *Journal of Autism and Developmental Disorders, 17*, 187–200.

Koegel, R. L., & Koegel, L. K. (1996). *Teaching children with autism*. Baltimore: Paul H. Brooks.

Kohen, D., Uppal, S., Guevremont, A., & Cartwright, F. (2007a). *Are 5 year old children ready to learn at school? Family income and home environment contexts*. Retrieved June 17, 2006, from http://www.statcan.ca/bsolc/english/bsolc?catno=81-004-x

Kohen, D., Uppal, S., Guevremont, A., & Cartwright, F. (2007b). *Children with disabilities and the educational system: A provincial perspective*. Retrieved June 17, 2006, from http://www.statcan.ca/ bsolc/english/bsolc?catno=81-004-x

Kohler, F. W., Anthony, L. J., Steiger, S. A., & Hoyson, M. (2001). Teaching social interaction skills in the integrated preschool: An examination of naturalistic tactics. *Topics in Early Childhood Special Education, 21*(2), 93–103.

Kola-Olusanya, A. (2005). Free-choice environmental education: Understanding where children learn outside of school. *Environmental Education Research, 11*(3), 297–307.

Kolic'-Vehovec, S., & Bajsanski, I. (2007). Comprehension monitoring and reading comprehension in bilingual students. *Journal of Research in Reading, 30*(2), 198–211.

Kontos, S., Moore, D., & Giorgetti, K. (1998). The ecology of inclusion. *Topics in Early Childhood Special Education, 18*, 1–38.

Kravits, T. R., Kamps, D. M., Kemmerer, K., & Potucek, J. (2002). Brief report: Increasing communication skills for an elementary-aged student with autism using the picture exchange communication system. *Journal of Autism Developmental Disorders, 32*(3), 225–230.

Kruse, C. K ., & Card, J. A. (2004). Effects of a conservation education camp program on campers' self-reported knowledge, attitude, and behavior. *The Journal of Environmental Education, 35*(4), 33–45.

REFERENCES

Kuoch, H., & Mirenda, P. (2003). Social story intervention for young children with autism spectrum disorders. *Focus on Autism and other Developmental Disabilities, 18*(4), 219–227.

Laa & Family. (2007). *Mom embracing autism.* Retrieved March 1, 2008, from http://momembracingautism. blogspot.com/2008/02/nature-study-birdwatching.html

Lattal, K. A., & Neef, N. A. (1996). Recent reinforcement: Schedule research and applied behavioral analysis. *Journal of Applied Behavior Analysis, 29*(2), 213–230.

Li, G. (2007). *Behavioral assessment report for Brandon Osei.* Toronto, Ontario, Canada: Toronto District School Board.

Lifshen, L., & Cole, E. (1999). *Behavioral assessment report for Brandon Osei.* Toronto, Ontario, Canada: Toronto District School Board.

Ling, J. (2002). *Speech and language report for Brandon Osei.* Toronto, Ontario, Canada: Toronto District School Board.

Lipps, G., & Yipton-Avila, J. (1999). *From home to school: How Canadian children cope* (No.89 F0117XIE.). Toronto, Ontario, Canada: Ministry of Culture and Tourism and the Centre for Education Statistics.

Littleton, D. (1991). *Influence of play settings on preschool children's music and play behaviors.* Unpublished doctoral dissertation, University of Texas, Austin.

Louv, R. (2006). *Last child in the woods.* New York: Algonquin Books of Chapel Hill.

Louv, R. (2008). *Last child in the woods.* New York: Algonquin Books of Chapel Hill.

Lovaas, O. I. (1967). A behavior therapy approach to the treatment of childhood schizophrenia. *Minnesota Symposia on Child Psychology, 1,* 108–159.

Lovaas, O. I. (1977a). *Behavior modification: Teaching language to psychotic children [CD].* New York: Appleton-Century-Crofts.

Lovaas, O. I. (1977b). *The autistic child: Language development through behavior modification.* New York: Irvington.

Lovaas, O. I., Koegel, R. L., Simmons, J. Q., & Long, J. (1973). Some generalization and follow-up and measures in autistic children behavior therapy. *Journal of Applied Behavior Analysis, 6*(1), 131–165.

Lovaas, O. I., Litronik, A., & Mann, R. (1971). Response latencies to auditory stimuli in autistic children engaged in self-stimulatory behavior therapy. *Behavior Research and Therapy, 9,* 39–49.

Lovaas, O. I., & Newsom, C. D. (1976). Behavior modification with psychotic children. In H. Leitenberg (Ed.), *Handbook of behavior modification and behavior therapy* (pp. 303–360). Englewood Cliffs, NJ: Prentice-Hall.

Lovaas, O. I., & Schreibman, L. (1971). Stimulus overselectivity of autistic children in a two-stimulus situation. *Behavior Research and Therapy, 9,* 305–310.

Lovaas, O. I., Koegel, R. L., & Schreibman, L. (1979). Stimulus over selectivity in autism: A review of research. *Psychological Bulletin, 86*(6), 1236–1254.

Lovaas, O. I., Koegel, R. L., Simmons, J. Q., & Long, J. (1973). Some generalization and follow-up & measures in autistic children behavior therapy. *Journal of Applied Behavior Analysis, 6,* 131–136.

Lovaas, O. I., Schreibman, L., Koegel, R. L., & Rehm, R. (1979). Selective responding by autistic children to multiple sensory input. *Journal of Abnormal Psychology, 77,* 211–222.

Lucas, A. (1979). *Environment and environmental education: Conceptual issues and curriculum implications.* Melbourne, Australia: Australian International Press and Publications.

Lukas, K. E., & Ross, S. R. (2005). Zoo visitor knowledge and attitudes toward gorillas and chimpanzees. *The Journal of Environmental Education, 36,* 4–33.

Makin, K. (2005a, April 4). Ontario discriminates against parents, students with autism, Judge rules. *The Globe and Mail,* p. A 1.

Makin, K. (2005b, February 2). Autism therapy vital, Ontario judge rules. *The Globe and Mail,* p. A 6.

Makin, K. (2006, July 8). Ontario appeal court upholds restricting of autism treatment. *The Globe and Mail,* p. A 6.

Marks, D. (1999). Dimensions of oppression: Theorizing the embodied subject. *Disability & Society, 14*(5), 611–626.

Marjoribanks, K., & Mboya, M. (2004). Learning environments, goal orientations, and interest in music. *Journal of Research in Music Education, 52*(2), 155–166.

Matthews, C. L. (2000). No known destination: Pre-primary music and Reggio Emilia. In *Spotlight on early childhood music education* (pp. 20–22). Reston, VA: National Association for Music Education.

McCabe, J., McCabe, J., & McCabe, E. (2003). *Living and loving with Asperger: Family viewpoints.* New York: Jessica Kingsley.

McConnell, S. R. (2002). Interventions to facilitate social interaction for young children with autism: Review of available research and recommendations for educational intervention and future research. *Journal of Autism and Developmental Disorders, 32*(5), 351–372.

McKeown-Ice, R., & Dendinger, R. (2000). Socio-political-cultural foundations of environmental education. *The Journal of Environmental Education, 31*(4), 37–45.

Minshew, N. J. (2001). The core deficit in autism and autism spectrum disorders. *Journal of Developmental and Learning Disorders, 5*(1), 107–118.

Minshew, N. J., & Goldstein, G. (1993). Is autism an amnesiac disorder? Evidence from the California Verbal Learning Test. *Neuropsychology, 7,* 209–216.

Miranda, M. L. (2004). The implication for development appropriate practice for kindergarten general music classroom. *Journal of Research in Music Education, 52*(1), 43–63.

Moore, M. (Ed.). (2000). *Insider perspectives on inclusion: Raising voices, raising issues.* Sheffield, England: Philip Armstrong Press.

Muller-Schwartze, D. (1984). *The behavior of penguins: Adapted to ice and tropics.* Albany, NY: University of New York.

Music. (2008). In *Merriam-Webster Online Dictionary.* Retrieved December 2, 2008, from http://www.merriam-webster.com/dictionary/music

Myles, B. S., Simpson, R. L., Ormsbee, C. K., & Erickson, C. (1993). Integrating preschool children with autism with their normally developing peers: Research findings and best practices recommendations. *Focus on Autistic Behavior, 8,* 1–18.

National Research Council. (2001). *Educating children with autism.* Washington, DC: National Academy Press.

Neelly, L. P. (2001). Developmentally appropriate music practice: Children learn what they live. *Young Children, 56,* 32–37.

Nesterenko, T. (2008). *Regional behavioral team: Speech and language consultation Note.* Newmarket, Ontario, Canada: York Region School Board.

Noddings, N. (1984). *A feminine approach to ethics & education.* Berkeley, CA: University of California.

Noddings, N. (2005). *The challenge to care in schools.* New York: Teachers College.

O'Brien, G., & Pearson, J. (2004). Autism and learning disability. *Autistic Society, 8*(2), 125–140.

Ontario Ministry of Education. (2001). *Special education: A guide for special educators.* Retrieved September 20, 2007, from http://www.edu.gov.on.ca

Ontario Ministry of Education. (2007a). *Effective educational practices for students with autism spectrum disorders.* Toronto, Ontario, Canada: Queen's Printer.

Ontario Ministry of Education. (2007b). *Ontario student record (OSR): School reports for Brandon Osei.* Toronto, Ontario, Canada: Author.

Ontario Ministry of Education and Training. (2008). *Education Act R.S.O. 1990.* Retrieved November 25, 2008, from http://www.e-laws.gov.on.ca/html/statutes/english/elaws_statutes_90e02_e.htm

Ontario Ministry of Education and Training. (1998). *The Ontario curriculum: The arts grades 1–8.* Toronto, Ontario, Canada: Queen's Printer.

Organization for Economic Co-operation and Development. (2000). *Special needs education: Statistics and indicators.* Paris: OECD Centre for Educational Research and Innovation.

Overton, J. (2003). *Snapshots of autism: A family album.* New York: Jessica Kingsley.

Palmberg, I., & Kuru, J. (2000). Outdoor activities as basis for environmental responsibility. *Journal of Environmental Education, 31,* 4–32.

REFERENCES

Papaioannou, V. (1997). *Communication and hearing report.* Toronto, Ontario, Canada: The Hospital For Sick Children (HSC).

Paterson, K., & Hughes, B. (1999). Disability studies and phenomenology: The carnal politics of everyday life. *Disability & Society, 14*(5), 597–610.

Peters, S., & Chimedza, R. (2000). Conscientization and the cultural politics of education: A radical minority perspective. *Comparative Education Review, 44*(3), 245–271.

Pratt, C., Lantz, J., & Loftin, R. (2002). Practical recommendations for utilizing a range of instructional approaches in general education settings. *Reporter, 7*(3), 1–11.

Prezant, F. P., & Marshak, L. (2006). Helpful actions seen through the eyes of parents of children with disabilities. *Disability & Society, 21*(1), 31–45.

Reichle, J., & Sigafoos, J. (1991). Establishing an initial repertoire of requesting. In J. Reichle, J. York, & J. Sigafoos (Eds.), *Implementing augmentative and alternative communication strategies for learners with severe disabilities* (pp. 89–114). Baltimore: Brookes.

Reichle, J., & Wacker, D. P. (Eds.). (1993). *Communicative alternatives to challenging behavior: Integrating functional assessment and intervention strategies.* Baltimore: Brookes.

Reid, D. (2008). *A sick baby sparks a father's research.* Retrieved February 19, 2008, from http://campusapps.fullerton.edu/news/research/2003/print/research.html

Reiff, H. B. (2004). Reframing the learning disabilities experience redux. *Learning Disabilities Research & Practice, 19*(3), 185–198.

Rimland, B. (1987). *Evaluation of the Tokyo Higashi program for autistic children by parents of the international division students.* Unpublished manuscript, the Tokyo Higashi School, Boston.

Rizzolatti, G., Fogassi, L., & Gallese, V. (2006). Mirrors in the mind. *Scientific American, 295*(5), 54–69.

Roberts, B. (2008). *Spring fun for kids: Spring poems.* Retrieved November 25, 2008, from http://www.bethanyroberts.com/BirdPoems.htm

Romanczyk, R. G. (1996). Behavioral analysis and assessment. In C. Maurice, G. Green, & S. Luce (Eds.), *Behavioral intervention for young children with autism* (pp. 195–217). Austin, TX: Pro-ed.

Ryan, M. (1995). One cure doesn't fit all. *The Advocate-Newsletter of the Autism Society of America.* Retrieved July 23, 2006, from http://www.autismlink.com/pages/autism_articles/

Sacks, O. (1985). *The man who mistook his wife for a hat.* New York: Touchstone.

Saegusa, T. (1991). The providence of nature: Teaching autistic children. *The Educational Forum, 55*(2), 139–153.

Sarnthein, J., vonStein, A., Rappeisberger, P., Petsche, H., Rauscher, F., & Shaw, G. (1997). Persistent patterns of brain activity: An EEG coherence study of the positive effect of music on spatial-temporal reasoning. *Neurological Research, 19*, 107–116.

Schopler, E. (1964). On the relationship between early tactile experiences and the treatment of an autistic and a schizophrenic child. *American Journal of Orthopsychiatry, 34*, 339–340.

Schopler, E., Lansing, M., & Walters, L. (1983). *Individualized assessment and treatment for autistic and developmentally disabled children.* Baltimore: University Park Press.

Schwartz, I. S., Garfinkle, A. N., & Bauer, J. (1998). The picture exchange communication system: Communicative outcomes for young children with autism. *Topics in Early Childhood Education, 18*(3), 144–159.

Scott, R. A. (1969). *The making of blind men.* New York: Russell Sage.

Shakespeare, T., & Watson, N. (2001). The social model of disability: An outdated ideology? In S. Barnartt & B. Altman (Eds.), *Exploring theories and expanding methodologies: Where we are and where we need to go* (Vol. 2, pp. 9–28). Stamford, CT: JAI Press.

Shea, V. (2004). A perspective on the research literature related to early intensive behavioral intervention (Lovaas) for young children with autism. *The National Autistic Society, 8*(4), 349–367.

Shepard, P. (1982). *Nature and madness*. Athens, GA: University of Georgia.

Shepardson, D. P. (2005). Student ideas: What is an environment? *The Journal of Environmental Education, 36*, 4–49.

Shipley, C. (2007). Our baby zebra has a new name. *The Toronto Public Zoo*. Retrieved June 12, 2007, from http://torontozoo.com/AboutTheZoo/PressRoom.asp?prs=20060914

Skinner, B. F. (1938). *The behavior of organisms*. New York: Appleton-Century-Crofts.

Sidebotham, P. (2003). The doctor, the father, and the social scientist. *Archives of Disease in Childhood, 88*(1), 44–44.

Simmons, M. (2000). *Individual education plan (IEP) for Brandon Osei*. Toronto, Ontario, Canada: Toronto District School Board.

Sinclair, J. (2004). *This is the place where I tell you about my autism*. Retrieved March 29, 2007, from http://www.angelfire.com/in/AspergerArtforms/autism.html

Smits, T. (2003). *Individual education plan for Brandon Osei*. Toronto, Ontario, Canada: Toronto District School Board.

Smithrim, K. L. (1997). Free musical play in early childhood. *Canadian Music Educators, 38*(4), 17–22.

Smith-Sebasto, N. J., & Semrau, H. (2004). Evaluation of the environmental education program at the New Jersey School of Conservation. *The Journal of Environmental Education, 36*(1), 3–18.

Snell, M. E., & Farlow, L. J. (1993). Self-care skills. In M. E. Snell (Ed.), *Instruction of students of students with severe disabilities* (4th ed., pp. 380–441). New York: Merrill.

Starr, E., Szatmari, P., Bryson, S., & Zwaigenbaum. (2003). Stability and change among high-functioning children with pervasive developmental disorders: A 2 year outcome study. *Journal of Autism and Developmental Disorders, 33*(1), 15–22.

Sue, R. (1999). The assessment of the child with autism: A family perspective. *Clinical Child Psychology, 4*(1), 63–78.

Sue, T. (2003). *Individual education plan for Brandon*. Toronto, Ontario, Canada: Toronto District School Board.

Swadener, B. B., & Lubeck, S. (1995). The social construction of children and families at risk: An introduction. In B. B. Swadener & S. Lubeck (Eds.), *Children and families at promise: Deconstructing the discourse of risk* (pp. 17–49). Albany, NY: State University of New York Press.

Tager-Flusberg, H., Joseph, R., & Folstein, S. (2001). Current directions in research on autism. *Mental Retardation and Developmental Disabilities Research Reviews, 7*, 21–29.

Tarski, C. (2007). *Building birdfeeders*. Retrieved June 15, 2007, from http://birding.about.com/library/weekly/aa032000b.htm

Teacher Focus Forum. (2006). *Michelle Dawson (person with autism) says ABA is a failure*. Retrieved August 11, 2008, from http://www.teacherfocus.com/phpBB2/viewtopic.php?t=5677

Terrace, H. S. (1963). Discriminating learning with and without errors. *Journal of the Experimental Analysis of Behavior, 6*, 1–27.

Thanh Ha, T. (2007, May 25). French and English look different to babies. *The Globe and Mail*. Retrieved from http://www.theglobeandmail.com/servlet/story/RTGAM.20070525.wlanguage25/BNStory/Science/

The Canadian Press. (2006, September 20). Horses help kids with disabilities. *Toronto 24 Hours*, p. L23.

The College of Psychologists of Ontario. (2005). *Standards of professional conduct*. Retrieved March 11, 2007, from http://www.cpo.on.ca/members-of-thecollege/index.aspx?id=1206&ekmensel=12_sub menu_0_link_2

The Ministers' Autism Spectrum Disorders Reference Group. (2007). *Making a difference for students with autism spectrum disorders in Ontario schools: From evidence to action*. Toronto, Ontario, Canada: Queen's Printer.

The Ontario Superior Court of Justice. (2005). *Wynberg vs. Ontario (CanL118749)*. Toronto, Ontario, Canada: Ontario Superior Court.

Thomas, P. A., Krampe, E. M., & Newton, R. R. (2008). Father presence, family structure, and feelings of closeness to the father among adult African American children. *Journal of Black Studies, 38*(4), 529–546.

REFERENCES

Tidmarsh, L., & Volkmar, F. R. (2003). Diagnosis and epidemiology of autism spectrum disorders. *Canadian Journal of Psychiatry, 48*(8), 517–527.

Tupper, M. (1966). *No place to play.* New York: Chilton.

Turner, K., & Freedman, B. (2004). Music and environmental studies. *The Journal of Environmental Education, 36*(1), 45–53.

UNESCO (United Nations Educational, Scientific and Cultural Organization). (1980). *Environmental education in the light of the Tbilisi conference.* Paris: Author.

Ungerer, J. A., & Sigman, M. (1981). Symbolic play and language comprehension in autistic children. *American Academy of Child Psychiatry, 20*, 318–337.

United Nations International Children's Emergency Fund (UNICEF). (2007). *Convention on the rights of the child.* Retrieved September 9, 2007, from http://www.unicef.org/crc/

Uppal, S., Kohen, D., & Khan, S. (2006). *Education services and disable children. Health analysis and measurement group, Statistics Canada.* Retrieved February 22, 2008, http://www.statcan.ca/english/freepub/81-004-XIE/2006005/disachild.htm

U.S. Public Health Service. (2000). *Report of the Surgeon General's conference on children's mental health: A national action agenda.* Washington, DC: Department of Health and Human Services.

Valdivia, R. (1999). *The implications of culture on developmental delay.* ERIC Clearinghouse on Disabilities and Gifted Education. (Eric Document Reproduction Service No. ED438663)

Van Berckelaer-Onnes, I. A. (2003). Promoting early play. *Autism Society, 7*(4), 415–423.

Van Manen, M. (1990). *Researching lived experience.* Toronto, Ontario, Canada: The Althouse.

Varenne, H., & McDermott, R. (1999). Introduction. In H. Varenne & R. McDermott (Eds.), *Successful failure: The school America builds* (pp. 1–21). Boulder, CO: Westview Press.

Vaughan, C., Gack, J., Solorazano, H., & Ray, R. (2003). The effect of environmental education on schoolchildren, their parents, and community members: A study of intergenerational and inter-community learning. *The Journal of Environmental Education, 34*(3), 12–21.

Vaughan, M. (1973). *An investigation of the relationship among musical aptitude, musical creativity, and figural creativity.* Unpublished research report, University of Victoria, Victoria, British Columbia, Canada.

Volpe, R., Cox, S., Goddard, L., & Tilleczek, K. (1997). *Children's rights in Canada: A review of provincial policies.* Toronto, Ontario, Canada: The Dr. R. G. N. Laidlaw Research Centre, Ontario Institute for Studies in Education.

Vouloumanos, A., & Werker, J. F. (2007). Listening to language at birth: Evidence for bias for speech in neonates. *Developmental Science, 10*(2), 159–171.

Webster, P. (1977). A factor of intellect approach to creative thinking in music (Doctoral dissertation, Eastman School of Music, University of Rochester, New York). *Dissertation Abstracts International, 38*(6), 3136A.

Webster, P. (1992). Research on creative thinking in music: The assessment literature. In R. Coiwell (Ed.), *Handbook of research on music teaching and learning* (pp. 266–280). New York: Schirmer Books.

Wells, N. M. (2000). At home with nature effects of greenness on children's cognitive functioning. *Environmental and Behavior, 32*(6), 775–795.

Westwood, P. (2003). *Commonsense methods for children with special educational needs* (4th ed.). London: Routledge Falmer.

Wheeler, K., & Bijur, A. (2000). *Education for sustainable future.* New York: Kluwer Academic.

Wilder, L. K., Dyches, T. T., Obiakor, F. E., & Algozinne, B. A. (2004). Multicultural perspectives on teaching students with autism. *Focus on Autism and Other Developmental Disabilities, 19*(2), 105–113.

Willey, L. H. (1999). *Pretending to be normal: Living with Asperger's syndrome.* London: Jessica Kingsley.

Winton, P. J., & Turnbull, A. P. (1981). Parent involvement as viewed by parents of preschool handicapped children. *Topics in Early Childhood Special Education, 1*(3), 11–19.

Wolf, M., Risley, T., & Mees, H. (1964). Application of operant conditioning procedures to the behavior problems of an autistic child. *Behavior Research and Therapy, 1*, 305–312.

Woodward, B., & Hogenboom, M. (2002). *Autism: A holistic approach.* London: Floris Books.

Woodward, S. C., Fresen, J., Harrison, V. C., & Coley, N. (1996, July). *The birth of musical language*. A paper presented at the Seventh International Seminar of the Early Childhood Commission of International Society for Music Education, Winchester, England.

Yanchyshyn, C. (1998). *The Toronto District School Board District-Wide Special Education Assessment*. Toronto, Ontario, Canada: Ministry of Education.

Yong-Yeon K., Hsian-nan, L., & Sanda, A. I. (2000). *Fat penguins and imaginary penguins in perturbative QCD*. Retrieved September 18, 2007, from http://arxiv.org/abs/hep-ph/0004

A LETTER TO DORIS

Dear Doris

Together we have been parenting our son Brandon without much support, information, stories of other families' journeys, without much medical, educational or other resource help. It has been years of figuring out what to do next, what Brandon needs, how to help him develop to the best of his abilities, how to support him in school and to advise his teachers. As you know, I have been journaling, wondering, keeping records of what I have been feeling, wondering about, learning and doing. It is these records, these stories that I want to develop into a thesis/story that will help us to understand what we have been learning and doing through these years. This narrative will be used as data for my thesis to be reflected on but also in the long run could be information that will inform others such as the medical and educational people dealing with Autism. We have discussed how important this work is for us and for others.

I want to take this opportunity to thank you for being the supportive other parent and I also want your permission to use these artifacts, journals, notes as data for my thesis work.

I will ask you to read the thesis in process and when completed with the lenses of parent protector and advocate for Brandon.

Also, I need your help to assist me to explain to Brandon what I am doing. I would like you to be present and to facilitate the complicated communication process with Brandon. I will read to him some of the notes that I have written and will explain, the best way I can, that the stories about him and about me will be for others to read to learn about autism. I will tell him that we will be teaching parents and teachers about what it is like for a dad and a son to know how to have a good day and to learn new things.

The girls, our daughters aged 13 and 16, will not be a part of the research process other than they will be witnesses to the writing and incidentally mentioned as participants in family events that have happened. Our daughters are both good readers and will be invited to read any segments of the data and interpretations that involve them specifically. The same will be true for you. You will have access to the entire theses because of your responsibility as mother to all three children. Obviously, there are some stories that involve you and I request your permission to use these stories in my thesis. You have the option of not granting permission for anything that you would prefer not to be told about you, Brandon or the girls.

The purpose of my study is to share what we have learned together.

Sincerely,

Albert

APPENDIX B

THE UNITED NATIONS CONVENTION ON THE RIGHTS OF THE CHILD

The United Nations Convention on the Rights of the Child states in article 7 that children are entitled to education that allows them to promote their culture, innate abilities, individual judgment, and moral and social responsibility to enable them to become productive members of society (Unicef, 2007; Office of the United Nations High Commissioner for Human Rights, 1997). The emphasis on individual abilities and judgments demonstrates the importance of allowing autistic students to freely express themselves in pedagogy and for their self-expressions to be taken seriously by their teachers and peers. In order to offer autistic students such rights, they need to be engaged in creative and productive dialogue. In 1990, Canada signed the United Nations Convention on the Rights of the Child, (Volpe, Cox, Goddard, and Tilleczek, 1997).

APPENDIX C

THE CHARTER OF RIGHTS AND FREEDOMS

The Charter of Rights and Freedoms provides a constitutional framework to assist provincial governments and educators for the organization of education programs that provide equal opportunity to every school going resident in the country. The Ontario special education guidelines explain that in order for Ontario to meet this constitutional obligation, the provincial government has introduced the Ontario Education Act R.S.O. 1990, C.E, 2, as amended and normally referred to as the Education Act, as a working document to guide legislators, school boards, parents, educators and civic groups to agree on a concept of education that will help provincial schools to provide equitable education for every student in the province (Ontario, Ministry of Education, 2001).

APPENDIX D

PARENTAL ADVOCACY IN SPECIAL EDUCATION FOR CHILDREN WITH AUTISM SPECTRUM DISORDERS

Makin (2005a) reports that the recent Ontario Superior Court decision requesting school boards to fund a therapeutic educational program known as applied behavioral analysis (ABA) for students' 6 years and older has had far-reaching consequences on special education programs and services for students with autism in Ontario. The court citation: Wynberg v. Ontario filed under docket number: 00CV184608CM at the Superior Court of Justice in 2005 for 35 autistic students' from 30 Ontario families' claims that the school board is denying students with autism ABA and IBI therapeutic treatment packages (Gray, 2007).

Gray elaborates that the autistic students and their families claim they were being discriminated against under the Ontario Education Act R.S.O. 1990, C.E, 2, because the school boards were denying their autistic children ABA and IBI therapies that are considered effective and appropriate educational intervention programs necessary for autistic students to develop progressively in the public school system (Makin, 2005a). On a contrary judgment, the Ontario Superior Court ruled against ABA therapeutic intervention in schools as unnecessary, and there was no scientific evidence to support its concept and practices (Makin, 2005b).

The earlier Court decision favored the autistic students' on the grounds that school boards, on behalf of the government of Ontario, had violated the rights of autistic students under sections 15 and 7 of the Charter of Rights and Freedoms because the provincial government refuses to fund the ABA program for autistic students' (CanL11, 2005). Makin clarified that the Court felt the Ontario school board had "violated the constitutional rights and human dignity of autistic school children by denying them treatment they desperately need in order to cope and thrive" in the school system (Makin, 2005a). The court ruling follows earlier decision in favour of the school board rendered by the Ontario Supreme Court. In an earlier Supreme Court ruling, the court argued that, "provinces had no obligation to provide such treatment under the health-care system" (Makin, 2005b). These conflicting legal decisions have heightened the debate about what constitutes appropriate educational practice that could assist autistic students to develop productively like other students in the public school system.

APPENDIX E

THE TREATMENT AND EDUCATION OF AUTISTIC AND COMMUNICATION HANDICAPPED CHILDREN PROGRAM (TEACCH)

Schopler (1964) scholarly work, "On the relationship between early tactile experiences and the treatment of an autistic and a schizophrenic child," has given prominence to the treatment and education of autistic and communication handicapped children program (TEACCH). Schopler and Olley (1982) discuss a comprehensive education program for autistic children. The TEACCH program consists of experiential learning models instead of behavioral therapeutic treatment procedures to teach autistic children basic social skills such as self-care and language acquisition techniques. TEACCH advocates that the educational needs of autistic students cannot be adequately addressed without taking into consideration the autistic students cultural and family social interests (Schopler and Olley, 1982).

Schopler (1964) advocates experiential learning strategies such as building on students strengths and not on their weaknesses, and backed by cultural and family social networks as a means for increasing student's interest in pedagogy (Schopler, 1964). Schopler and Oiley (1982) argue that students are not likely to apply new skills from rigid behavioral rules and procedures in everyday settings, especially in language acquisition. The TEACCH program is a student-centered and teacher directed learning activity that allows the student to apply his or her own experience to solve the task at hand. The Ontario special education program puts students with autism anywhere from special education classroom to regular classroom without considering students experiences and abilities developed from their nature interactions.

The lack of information about students nature experiences have left the special education teacher little information to work with. Brandon nature experiences suggest that autistic students are more likely to produce better results when pedagogy is reflective on their lived experiences. In contrast to the ABA concept, the TEACCH project is designed to grant autistic students the opportunity to negotiate with the curriculum in a way that allows them to be pace-setters for their academic future. Schopler and Oiley contend that the TEACCH program could benefit students' with special needs such as autistic students by integrating them into a regular classroom setting that includes both normally developing and children with impairments.

Schopler and Oiley have asserted that segregated classrooms do not help students with special needs because they do not see or experience their normal developing peers in action in order to learn from them. This integrative and collaborative effort in special education raises very interesting issues relating to developing inclusive curriculum and classroom settings suitable for children with special needs.

What Schopler and Oiley refused to show is a verifiable and tested experimental account of the TEACCH concept to provide readers with information regarding workability, feasibility and practicality of putting children with autism in a regular classroom with their normally developing peers. Hodge reiterates that autistic students need clarity in areas of the curriculum where they will be asked to work, and this may involve planning and delivering materials and assignments that are well structured to provide the student with a high degree of independence as well as comfort and support.

APPENDIX F

THE UNITED NATIONS CONVENTIONS ON ENVIRONMENTAL EDUCATION (NATURE EDUCATION)

In 1972, the United Nations (UN) held its first international conference on environmental education (nature education) in Stockholm, Sweden to seek global consensus for organizing a global nature education strategy. This meeting was followed up with the Belgrade Conference in 1975. At the Belgrade meeting, the UN conference participants produced a charter describing a global consensus on a nature education framework. The Belgrade charter called for the establishment of International Environmental Education Program for the period covering 1975 to 1985. In 1977, the UN convened another meeting in Tbilisi (USSR) to begin Inter-governmental discussions on Environmental Education (UNESCO, 1977; UNESCO, 1978; UNESCO, 1980). The International Union for the Conservation of Nature (IUCN) introduced a report, Caring for the Earth, a global conservation strategy to accommodate the conservation of nature and economic development.

The idea was to allow economic exploitation of nature and nature conservation programs to coexist in nature education without any fundamental changes (IUCN, 1980). Many in the nature education community did not find the IUCN proposal realistic as a nature education strategy. The UN was compelled to come up with a new nature education framework that was consistent with present societal needs as well as future expectations. The World Commission on Environment and Development (WCED) prepared a new nature education strategy, Our Common Future, commonly referred to as the Brundtland Report in 1987 (WCED, 1987). Our Common Future discusses the concept of sustainable development. The educational strategy quickly became a buzzword for businesses, environmental educators, governments and civil society.

Our Common Future reports that critical global environmental problems were primarily the result of the enormous poverty in developing countries and the non-sustainable patterns of consumption and production in industrialized countries. The report calls for a nature education strategy that is sensitive to development as well as nature. The WCED document subscribes to sustainable development as development that meets the needs of the present without compromising the ability of future generations to meet their own needs. The report echoed the concerns of many in the nature education community in a way that encouraged the UN to organize the Earth Summit in Rio de Janeiro to discuss the WCED report in greater detail. This time, over 179 heads of governments agreed to a 21 point strategy to guide the implementation of the WECD educational strategy. The focal idea of the WECD framework was to put human interests at the core of a nature education framework. In fact, the WECD strategy encouraged many governments, including the Government of Canada, to introduce sustainable development in nature education discourse and practices in a way that was consistent with the Rio Declaration in 1992.

Shortly after the Rio conference, the Canadian government put into action the provision of the WECD framework by inviting nature educators, businesses, civil community groups and not for profit organizations to seek ways to implement the Rio protocol. In 1992, Environment Canada helped organized one of the largest nature education conferences in Toronto. There were participants from several countries and organizations in Canada. For example, there were educators, researchers, businesses, community leaders, media agencies, environmentalists and non-profit organizations such as the Canadian Network for Environmental Education and Communication (EECOM) that engaged dialogically about ways to implement the Rio declaration.

The Canadian government worked with nature education organizations (such as Learning for a Sustainable Future (LSF), a not-for-profit organization) to assist educators from across Canada to integrate the principles of sustainable development into national education strategy for schools. The proviso included internet-based sustainability education and technology programs such as The Hurley Island Project, to assist secondary school students across Canada to exchange ideas about a sustainable future for Canada. There were innovative pilot projects, such as pre-packaged nature education activities to meet the interests of students across Canada (like the Green Street project).

At the postsecondary level, the government coordinated with organizations such as the Canadian Consortium for Sustainable Development Research (CCSDR), and environmental education organizations and research institutions to develop nature education programs to focus on areas of sustainable development, biodiversity, conservation, environmental policy and environmental technology according to the Rio declaration (Environment Canada (a), 2006).

ECOPEDAGOGY

Integrating Nature and Environmental Education

We learn from Kahn (2003) that ecopedagogy represents a pedagogic effort to bring together ecological literacy and environmental education for the purpose of transforming traditional curricula by integrating information and strategies that are more sensitive to achieving nature literacy. Gadotti (2000), Jardine (2000), and Ahlberg (1998) treat ecopedagogy as a critical theory aimed at improving and expanding environmental and ecological education ideas to meet future challenges related to nature. In examining the dialogic quality of experience in nature and nature literacy, Kola-Olusanya has observed that nature interactions contribute to creative and productive early childhood experiences in nature education and also provides a vivid explanation of the diversity of abilities in childhood development.

According to Kola-Olusanya (2006), nature learning not only offers children a voice for self advocacy but explains the different environments where learning about the environment occurs in early childhood development. Palmberg and Kuru's (2000) study of students suggest that students' nature literacy offers self-confidence, a sense of safety and empathy for others. Nature learning motivates students to develop self-consciousness, relational understanding of others and understanding of one's place in the natural world. Shepardson (2005) identifies interest in nature and nature education as a way for students to develop self-awareness, relationships with others and interest in a sustainable planet.

For years, researchers have not been able to adequately investigate how nature and nature education could help autistic students to develop self-consciousness, relationships with others, and their place in the natural world. I believe that autistic students have an important role to play in the discursive subject of harnessing pedagogic ideas and environmental education for achieving environmental quality. Palmberg and Kuru (2000) have observed that nature and nature education could improve students' socialization with others and help them develop empathy for nature. Studies have suggested that autistic students do not demonstrate empathy for others. One of the most important contributions Ecopedagogy brings to this study is to connect various ecological and environmental ideas for the purpose of understanding Brandon's interest in nature and nature education. Such information will help educators and parents develop learning activities that focus on improving autistic students' social and academic work skills.

Leigh (2005) uses ecoautism as a psychopathic metaphor to identify the interconnectedness between humans and nature. According to Leigh, "Ecoautism represents a psychopathological metaphor where the human species has become autistic in relation to the natural world" (Leigh, 2005). Although Leigh does not refer to the lack of information about how autistic students develop relationship with the environment, his lucid use of the novel term reminds the research community to begin investigating a way to introduce nature and nature education to autistic students' learning programs. For example, nature and nature education could offer an opportunity for both teacher and student to share their personal interests about the environment.

GLOSSARY

Definition of Terms

Applied behavioral analysis (ABA): The concept is derived from extensive behavioral research, often with non-humans, but has gained popularity in applied therapy to identify behavioral differences in autistic students and students living with other developmental impairments. It is also used as a functional assessment tool for students with behavioural and emotional problems for classroom planning (Steege, 1999).

Autistic disorder: Involves significant impairment in social, communication and restricted range of activity and interests. There is significant variation in symptoms of the disorder according one's developmental level and chronological age. Autism spectrum disorder is commonly referred to as "early infantile autism, childhood autism, or Kanner's autism" (ASA, 1994; 70).

Cognitive skill: A term used to describe different ways for processing information to achieve a specific task.

Conscientization: is developing self-consciousness from lack of knowledge to knowledge of the world for the purpose of self-liberation (Freire, 1985, p. 168).

Ecopedagogy: Is a novice term that describes a holistic approach to ecological literacy for the benefit of the natural environment. Several educators have articulated the need to bring together ecological pedagogic strategies under a new set of trans-formative pedagogy that is free from imposition and manipulation to promote societal ecological consciousness. Ecopedagogy advocates that contemporary nature education pedagogies are inadequate as a solitary educational strategy for promoting progressive ecological attitudes towards nature (change from human negative actions to progressive and constructive relationship with nature).

Ecopedagogy is rooted in the ecological awareness that cultivates qualities of learning that go far beyond pedagogic imposition, excessive exploitation and manipulation as a means to promote a healthy planet Earth (Gadotti, 2000; Jardine, 2000). In this study, ecopedagogy represents a family's nature learning practices, experiences, values that have been transmitted between generations to inform my parenting practice. To put it simply, ecopedagogy captures the educational praxis of one family's ancestral learning practices and experiences that have come together in this study to inform and transform the learning experience of one autistic student in an urban school.

Educational development: Involves teaching, learning new skills, acquiring knowledge, critical thinking skills and wisdom. Education is also about passing cultural knowledge between generations (Freire, 2003). Educational development begins at birth and continues throughout life. Evidence suggests that education begins before birth through adulthood (Vouloumanos & Werker, 2007). For example, evidence indicates that playing music or reading to a baby in the womb could influence the child's social and cognitive abilities. Others contend that experiences of daily life provide far more experience than the formal school system.

Environmental education: Is the process of adopting values and clarifying concepts for the purpose of developing skills, and attitudes necessary to understand and appreciate the interconnectedness among humans, culture and the biophysical environment. It also involves developing decisions through research for educating human actions to achieve environmental quality (Gough, 1997).

Functional behavioral assessment (FBA): A behavioral assessment procedure that involves four levels of functional assessment: indirect assessment, descriptive assessment, brief functional analysis, and extended functional analysis. The assessment procedures draw substantial information from ABA principles (Steege, 1999).

Global developmental delay (GDD): Is when a child has delayed achievement of one or more developmental milestones, this is developmental delay. GDD implies that the child has delays in all areas of development (Bibic, 2007). According to the American Academy of Neurology and the Child Neurology Society of America, "between 40,000 and 120,000 U.S. and Canadian children are born each year with GDD (mental retardation)" (Alementi, 2003). While incurable, early testing and diagnosis could provide more accurate information about GDD and help researchers to determine the cause of the disorder and assist physicians and parents in developing a plan for treatment. GDD is prevalent in one to three percent of children less than five years of age.

Impairment: According to Statistics Canada (2007) from the early part of 1970, society's understanding of impairment has grown and societal shift from a "medical" to "social" construction of impairment has gained more ground. The Canadian Charter of Rights and Freedoms guarantees the rights of individuals with impairments as equal citizens.

The Charter has played a transformative role in education delivery and services for students' with social and cognitive impairment across Canada (Canada, 2005). The Charter advocates that children residents in Canada must have equal access to education and that their interest in education must be cultivated. In my conceptual analysis of one autistic student's urbanized schooling, I treat impairment and impairment as synonymous because both are socially constructed as a way for describing an oppressed and marginalized community.

Impulsive language: is a language spoken without thinking ahead.

Manipulative education: A system of education identified as cognitively invasive because it is education by imposition that treats people as receptors of information and not agents of transformation (Freire, 2003).

Nature: Refers to the various types of plant and animal species, and in some cases to the processes associated with inorganic systems. For example, the way particular types of things exist and change of overtime, such as the weather and geology of the Earth, matter and energy of which things are composed. Nature is often used interchangeably with the terms "natural environment" or "natural world" such as wild animals, rocks, forest, beaches, and things that have not been substantially altered by human exploitation or exist due to human interference. The traditional concept of nature can be found in many areas of the earth. Nature implies a distinction between the natural and the artificial environments.

Nature education: Involves developing values, critical thinking and engaging in actions that advance the interdependent and interconnected relationships between nature and humans. Nature education promotes the sustainable use of the planet and its resources (Wheeler and Bijur, 2000).

Pedagogy: Relates to the activity of teaching, parenting, educating or caring for children, that requires making decisions in situations and relations (Van Manen, 1990).

Pervasive developmental disorders (PDDs): Refer to severe and pervasive impairment in developing reciprocal social interaction in areas of verbal and non-verbal communication skills or with the presence of stereotypic behaviour, interest, and activities. Impairments that define these conditions are noticeably abnormal relative to individual development or mental age (APA, 1994). PDDs are some-times referred to as autism spectrum disorders (ASDs). PDDs consist of a spectrum of disorders: autistic disorder, Rett's disorder, Childhood disintegrative disorder, Asperger's disorder, and Pervasive developmental disorder, not otherwise specified. "These disorders are usually evident in the first years of life and are often associated with some degree of mental retardation" (APA, 2000; 69). PDD and autism are terms used interchangeably in this study to signify similarities relative to how Brandon has functioned in pedagogy.

Problem posing education: Refers to the constant production of knowledge within an environment that is free from imposition and domination. We learn from Freire (2003) that problem posing education is not manipulative because it does not recognize cognizable objects as private property.

Receptive language: Receptive language is the ability to comprehend information. It may include understanding of the vocabulary and concepts presented, short-term memory and sequencing information.

Social interactions skills: Refer to developing reciprocal relationship between peers based on a dynamic, changing sequence of social actions. For example, when a child demonstrates understanding for engaging a peer in turn-taking as a means for socializing. In other words, social relation skills are actions identifying social situations where people respond to each other amicably (Turnbull, Pereira & Blue-Banning, 1999).

Breinigsville, PA USA
23 December 2010
252081BV00004B/11/P